Relaxation

50 Unique Mandalas for Mindful Meditation

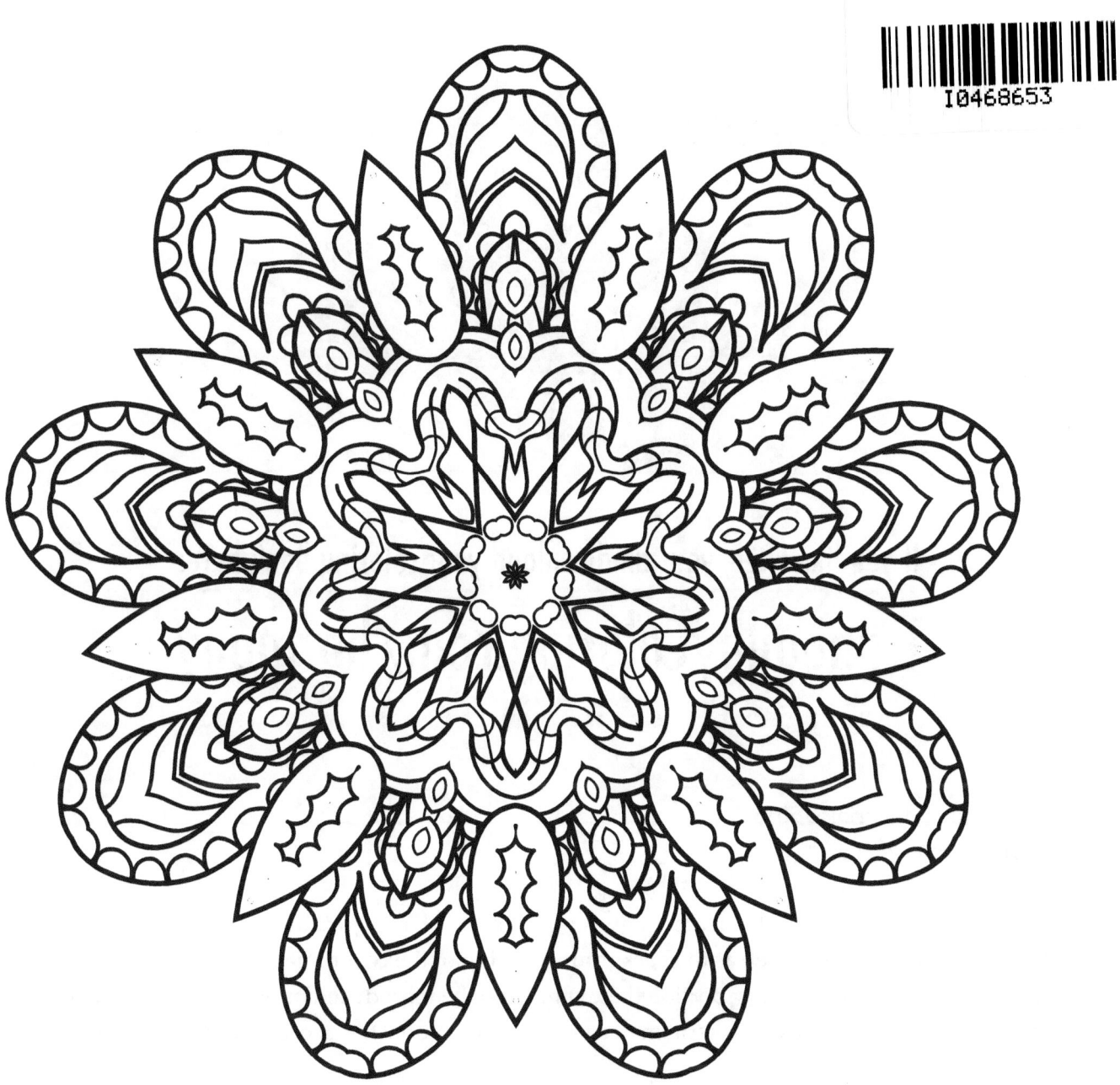

An Intricate Adult Coloring Book, Volume 5
by Talia Knight

TranquilityColoring.com

Want FREE coloring pages?

Talia Knight is giving away a free coloring book

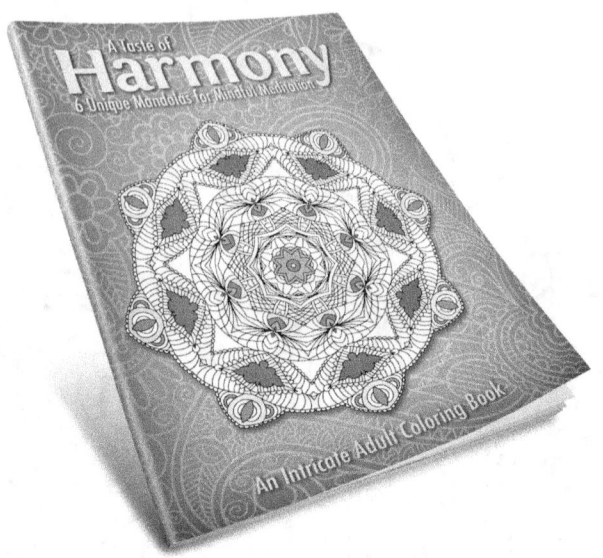

If you like <u>FREE</u>, you can download your coloring book here:

TranquilityColoring.com/harmony

ISBN-13: 978-1530953561   ISBN-10: 1530953561

Published by Tranquility Coloring
TranquilityColoring.com

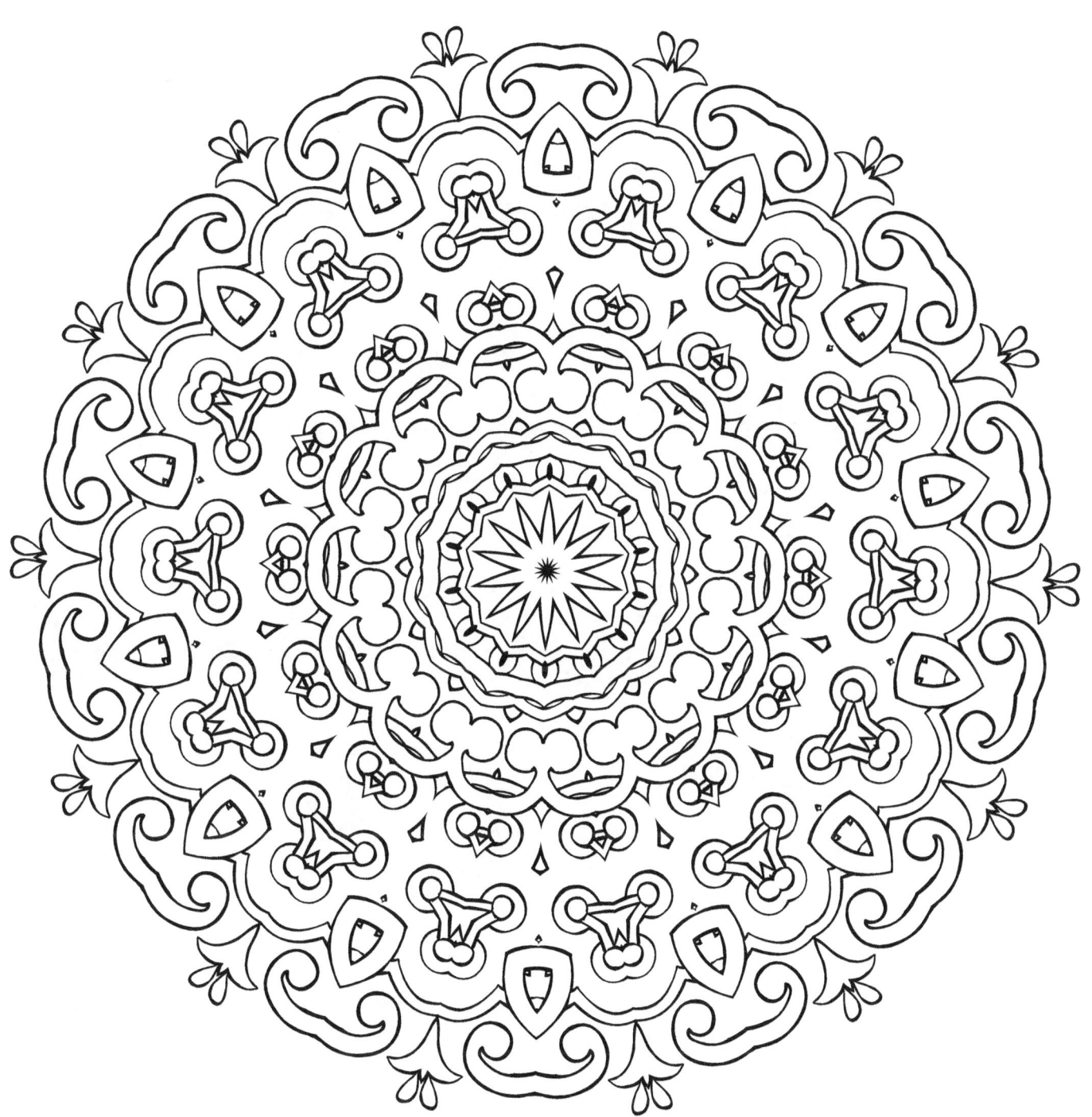

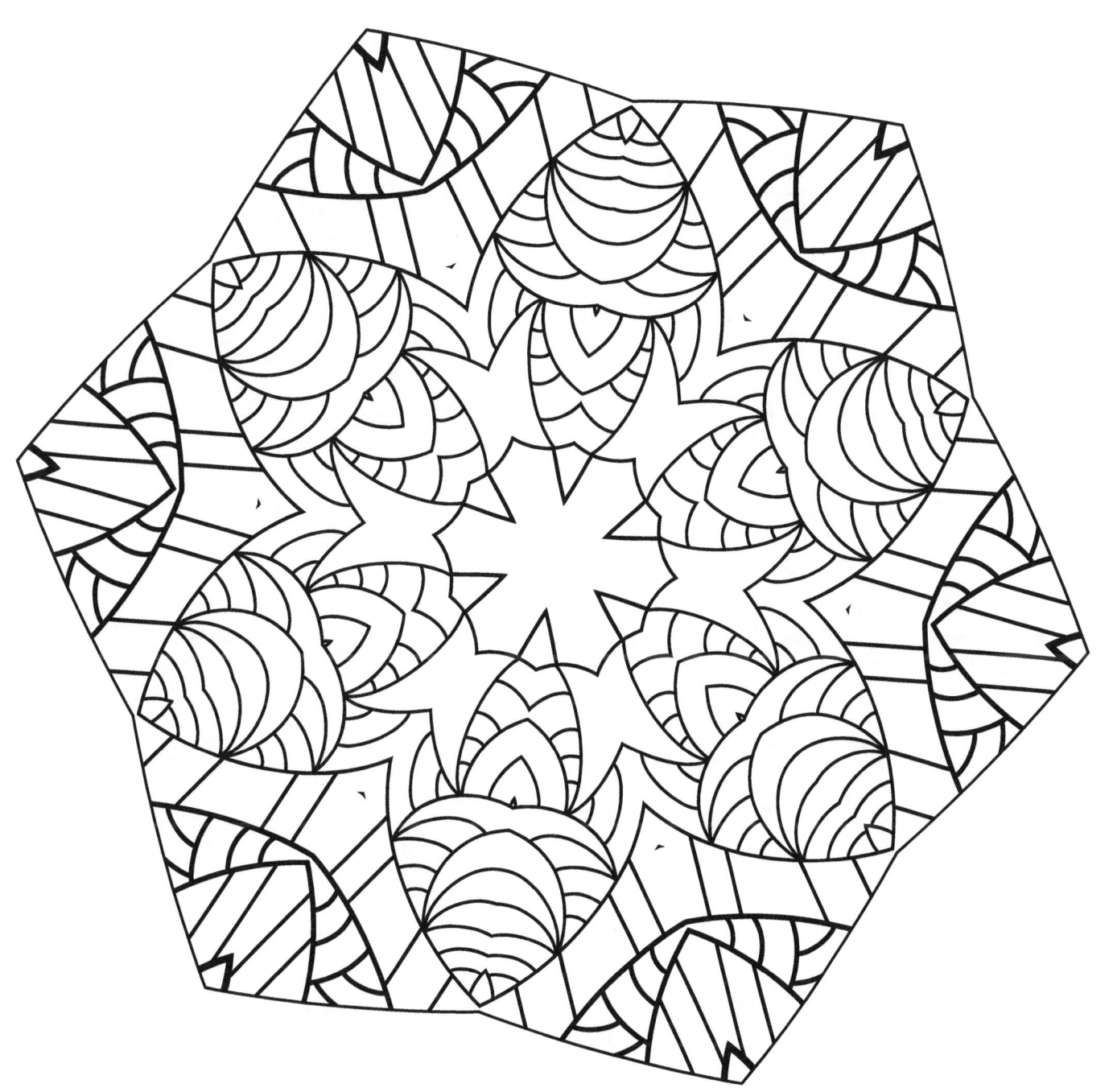

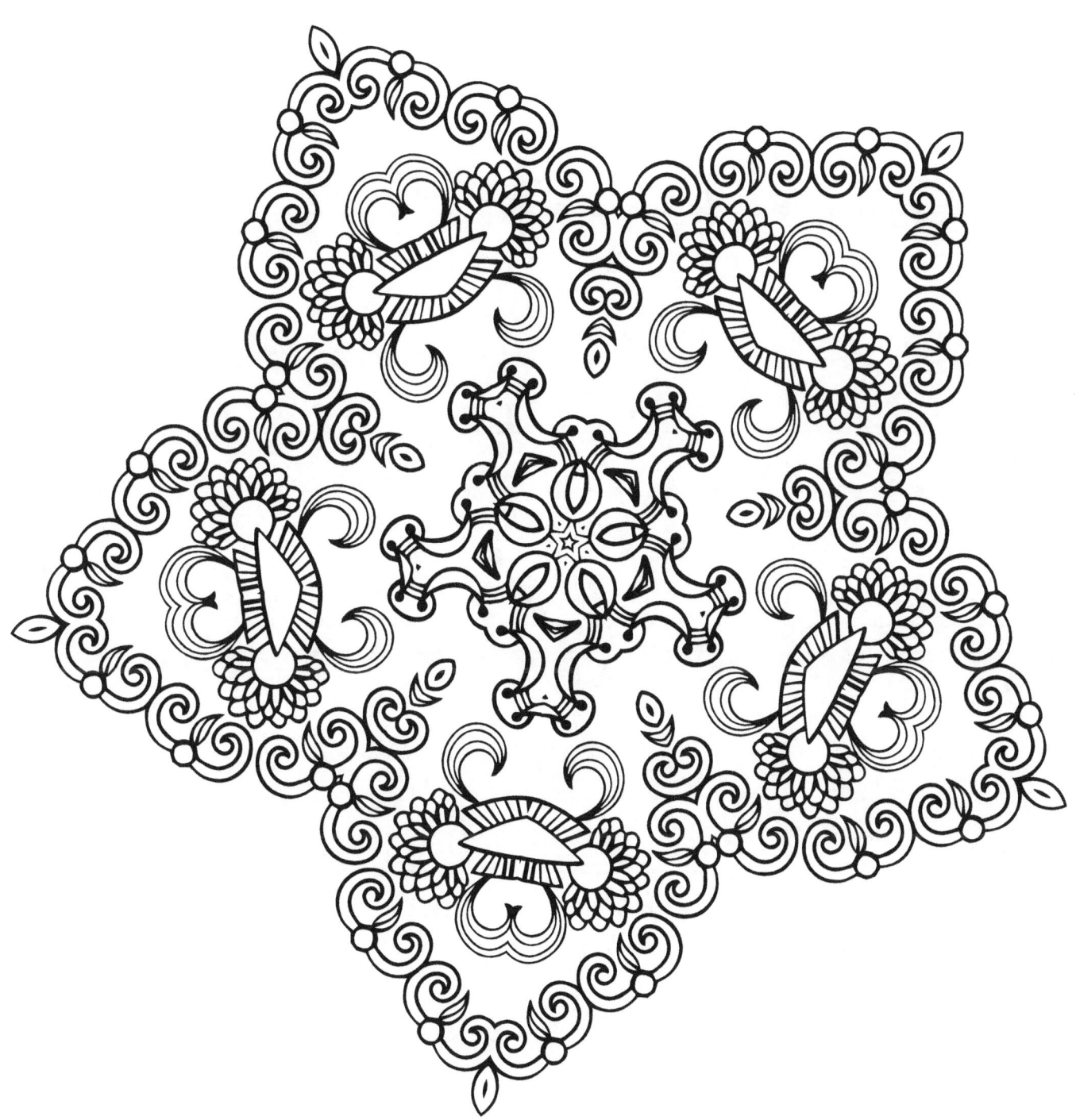

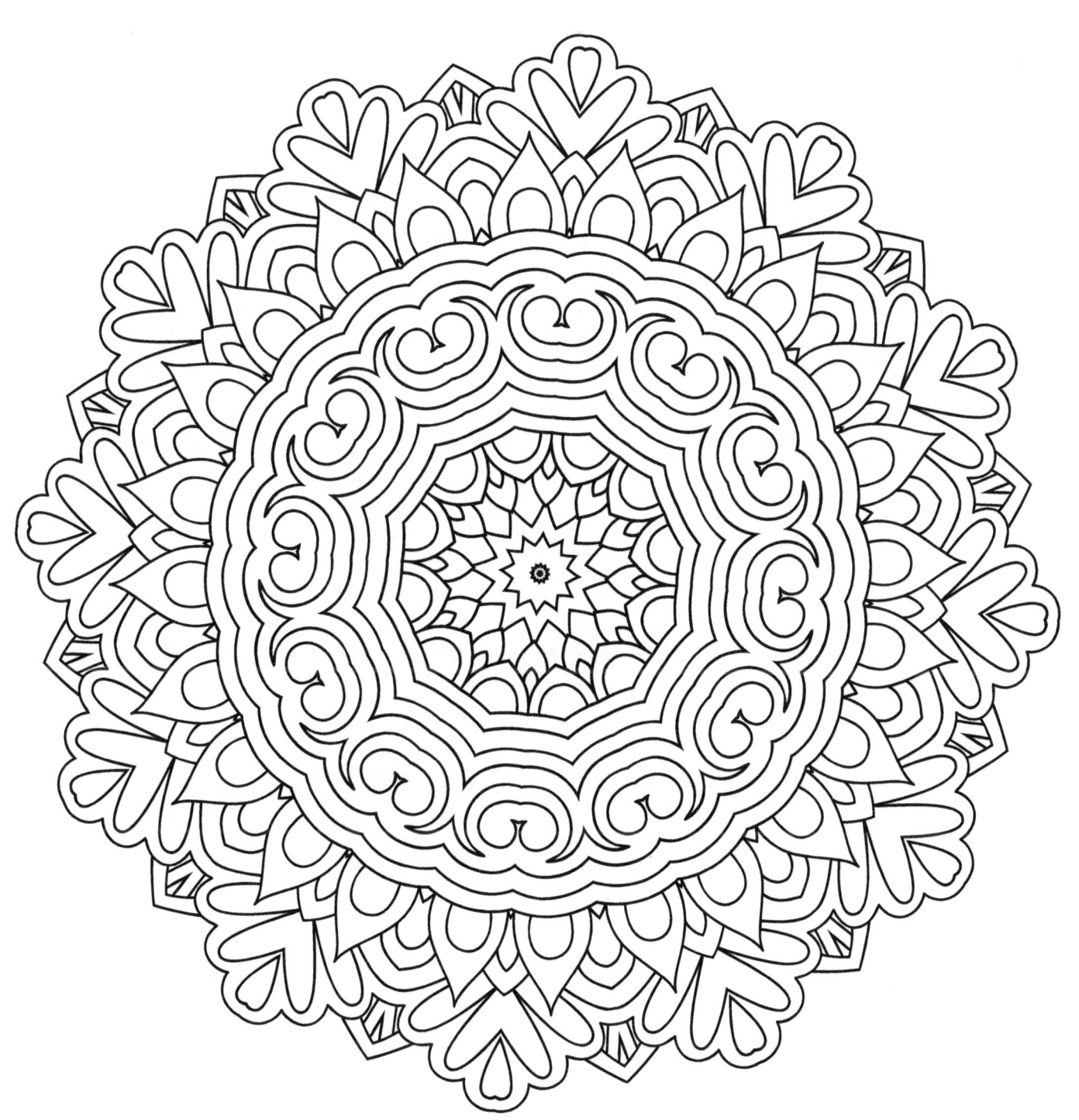

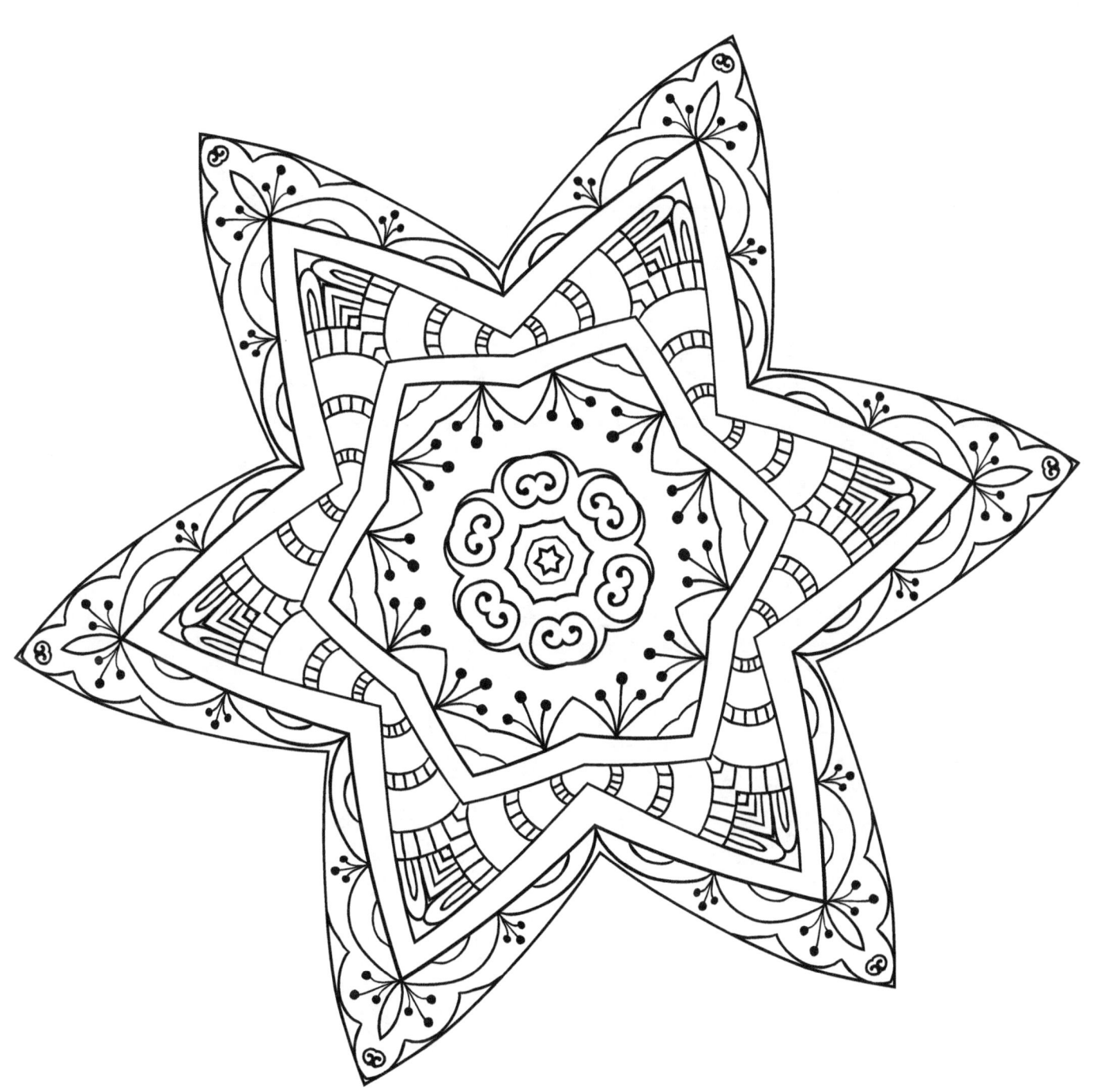

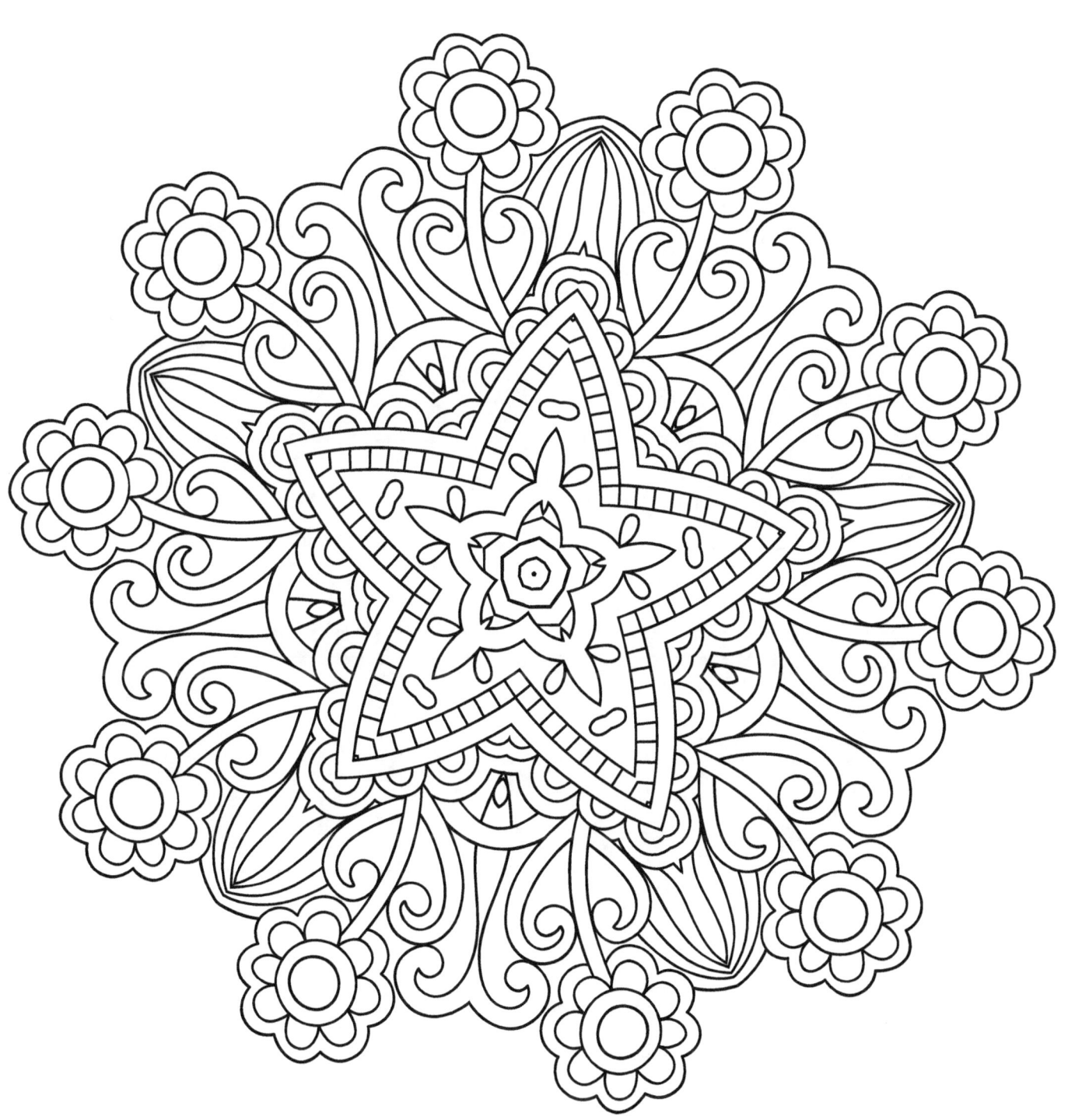

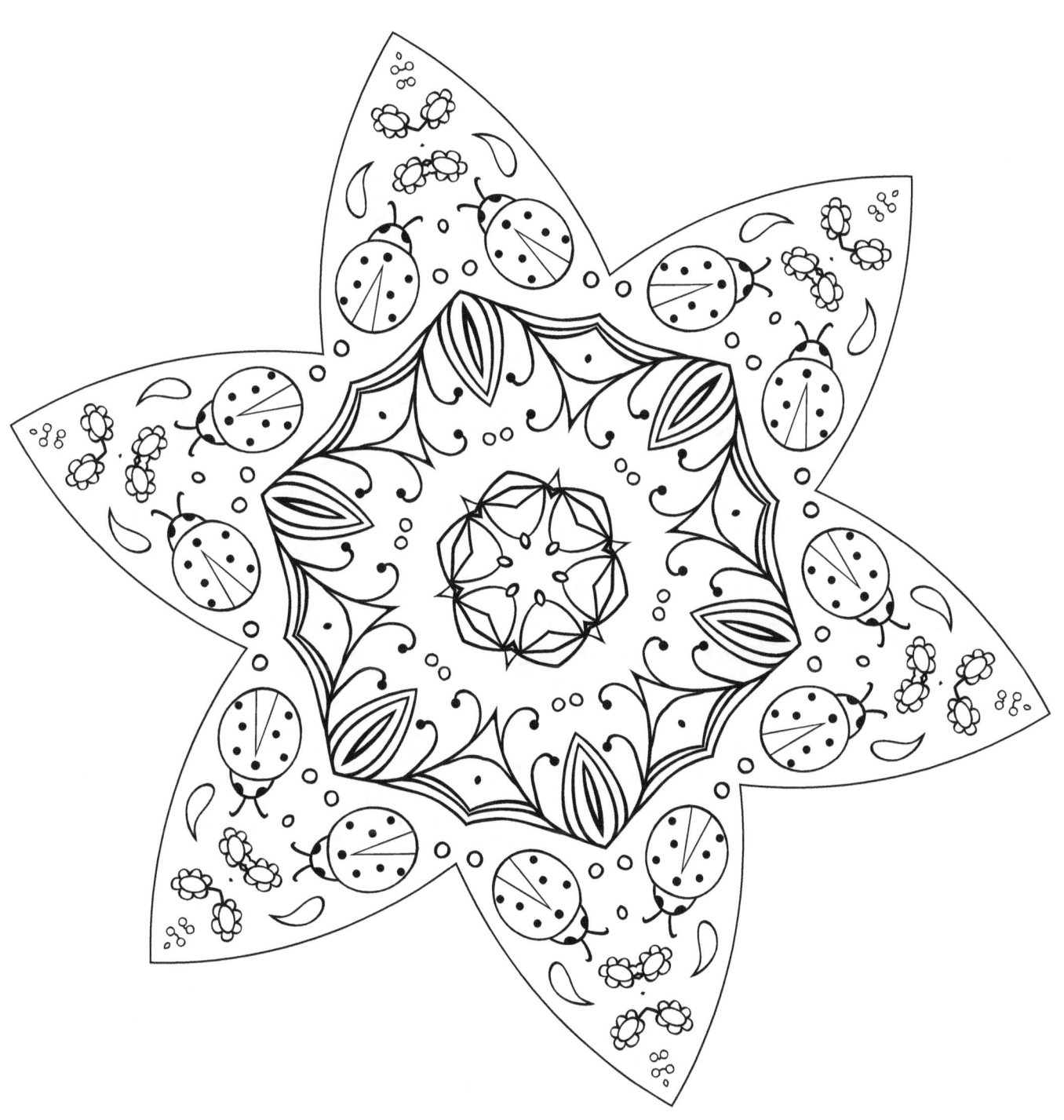

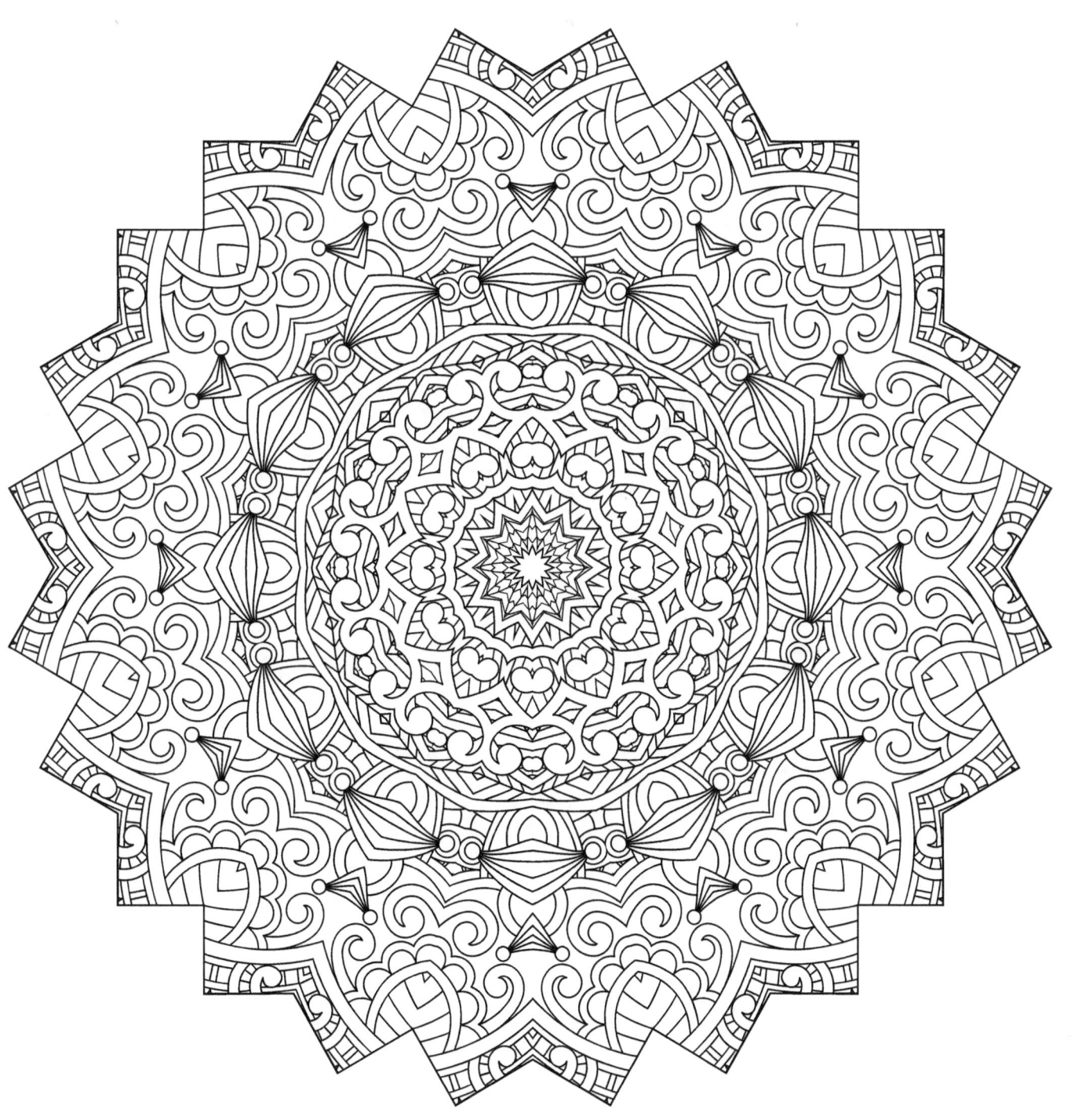

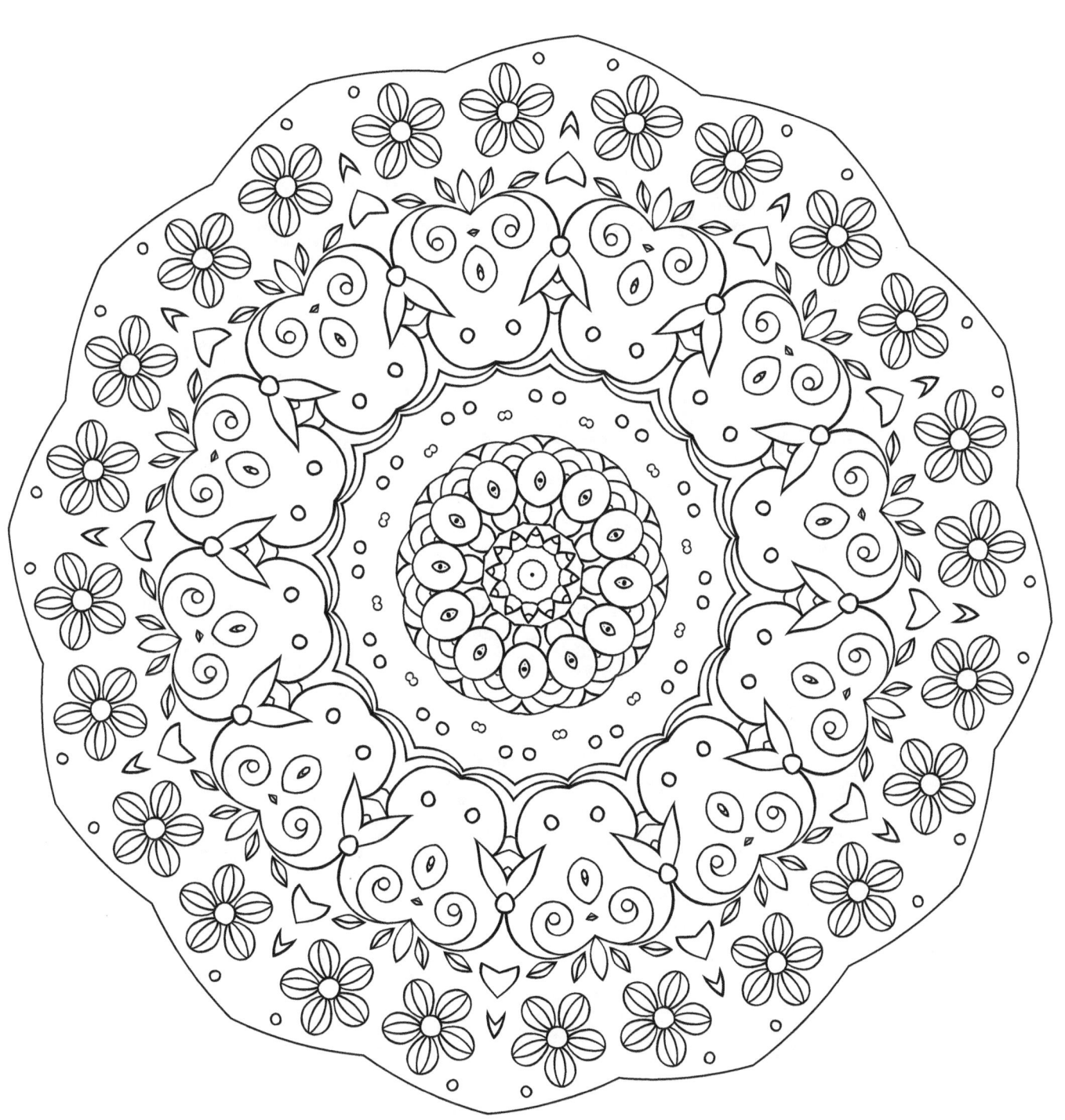

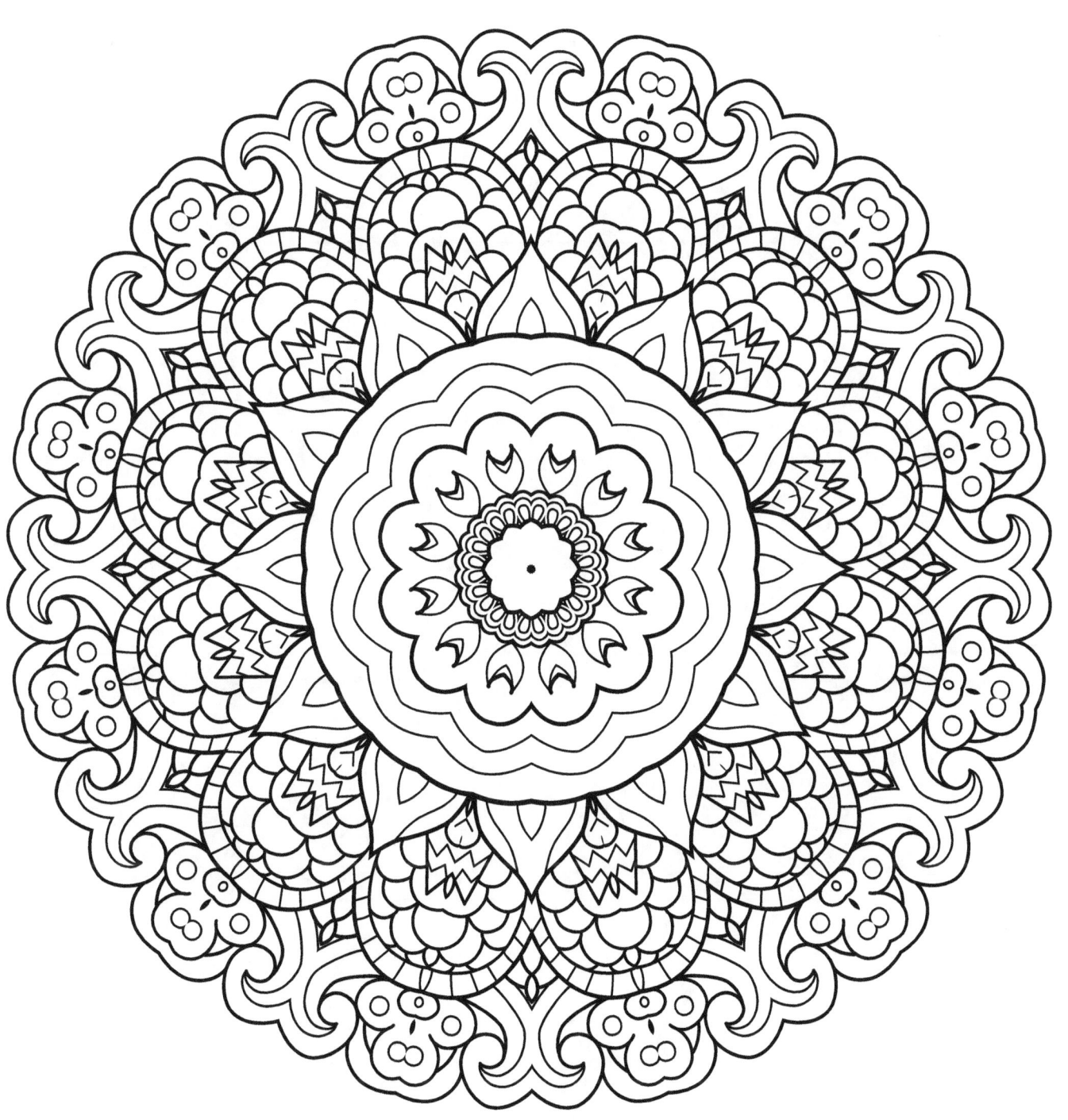

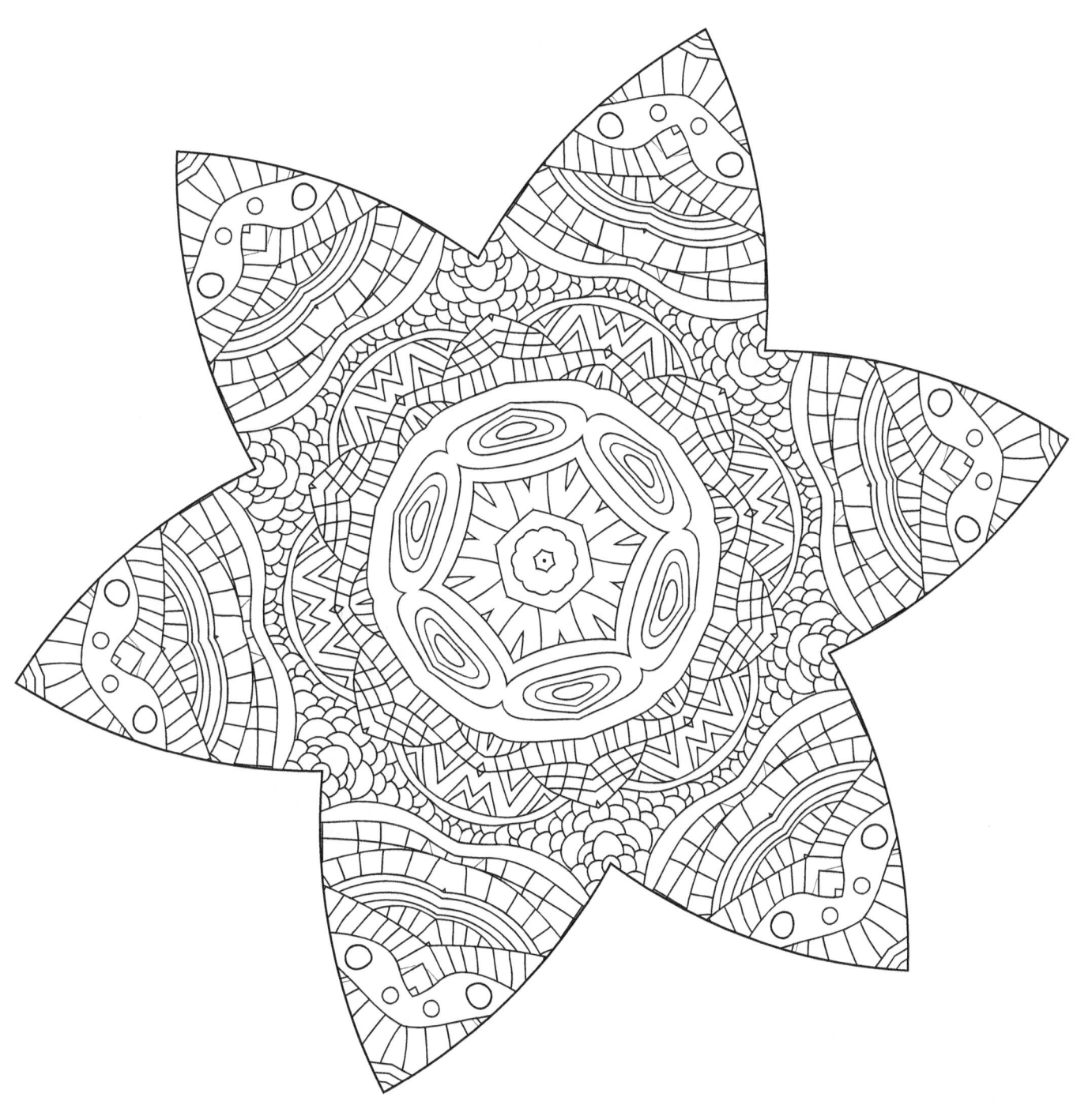

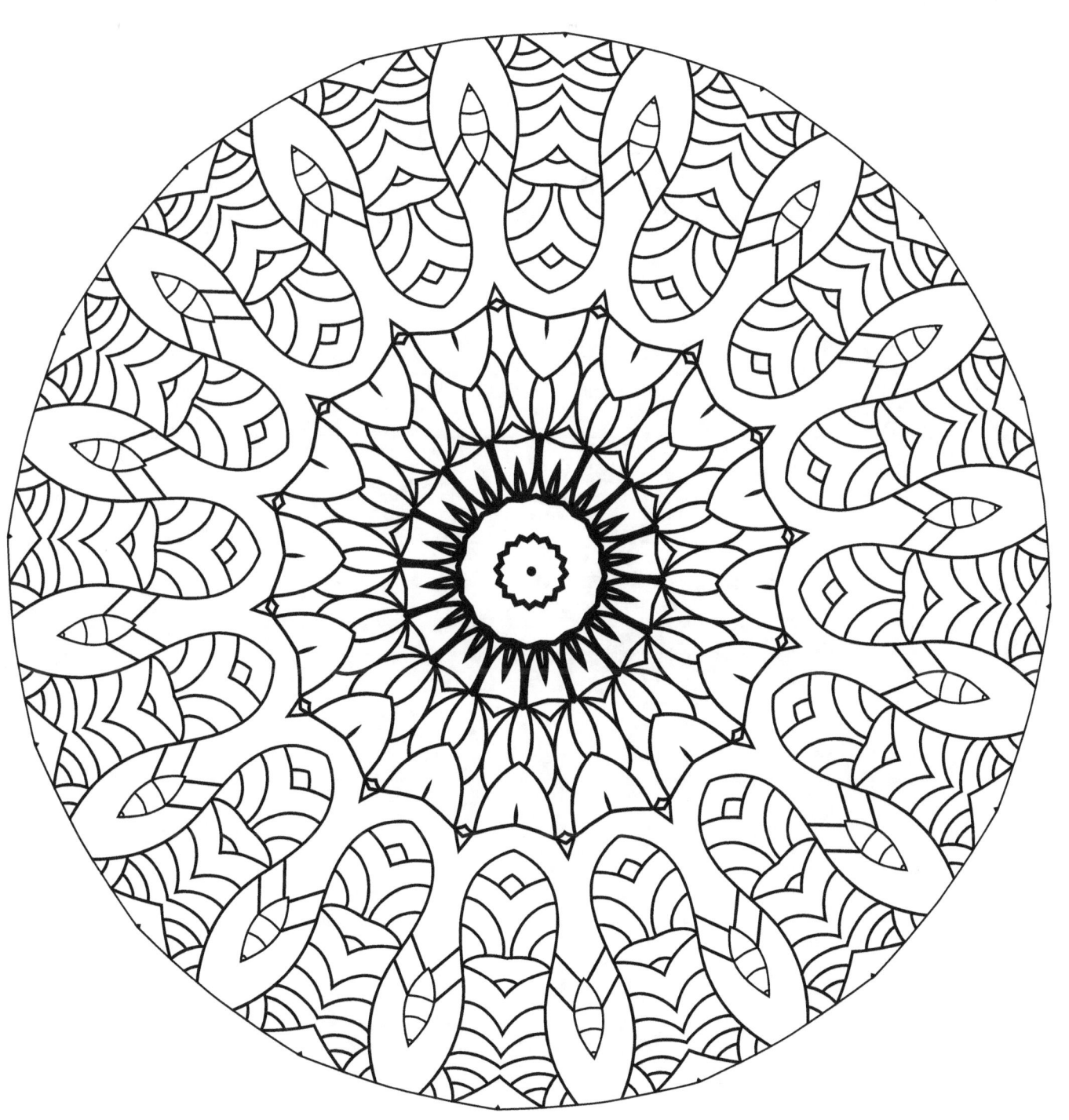

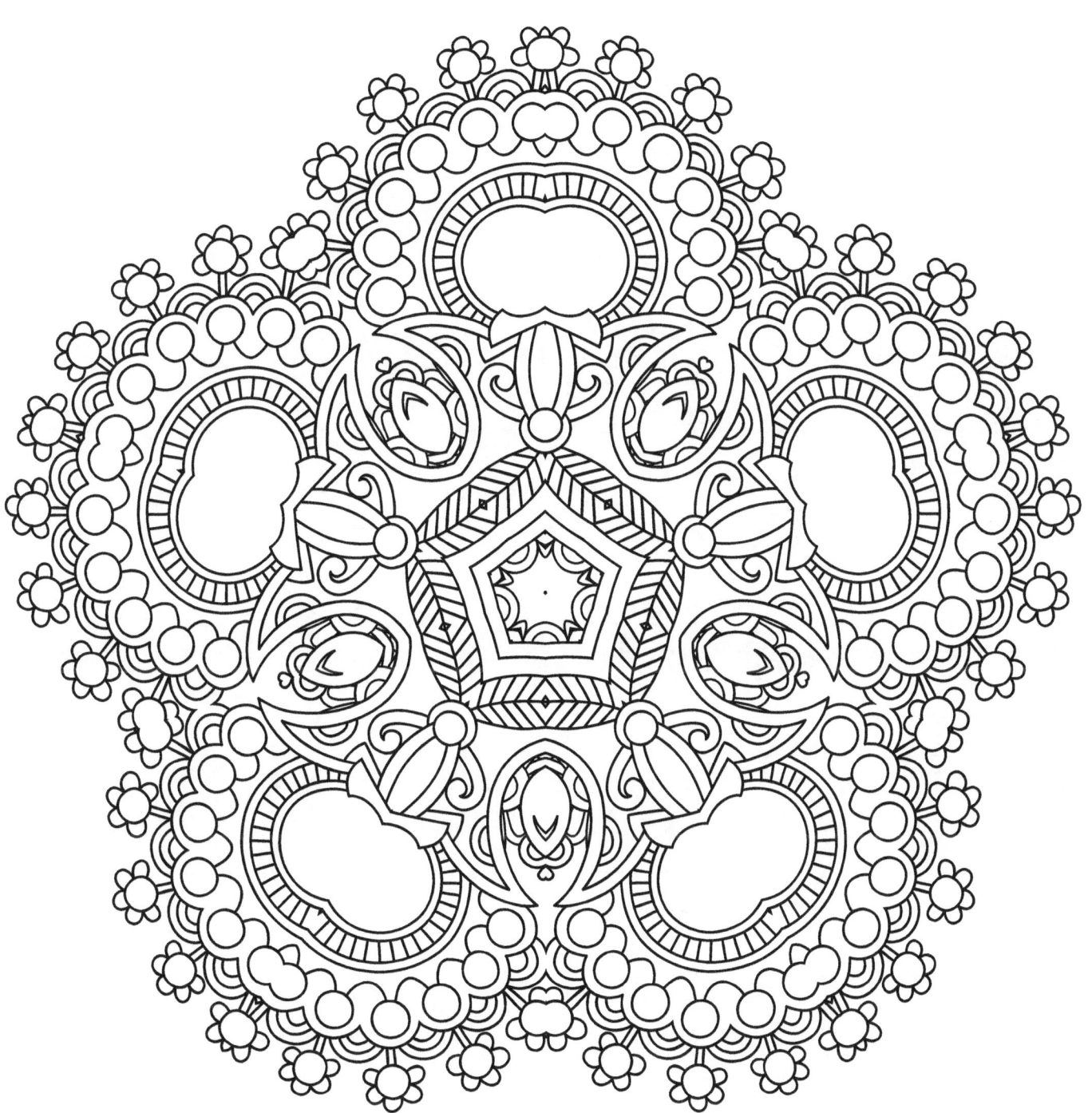

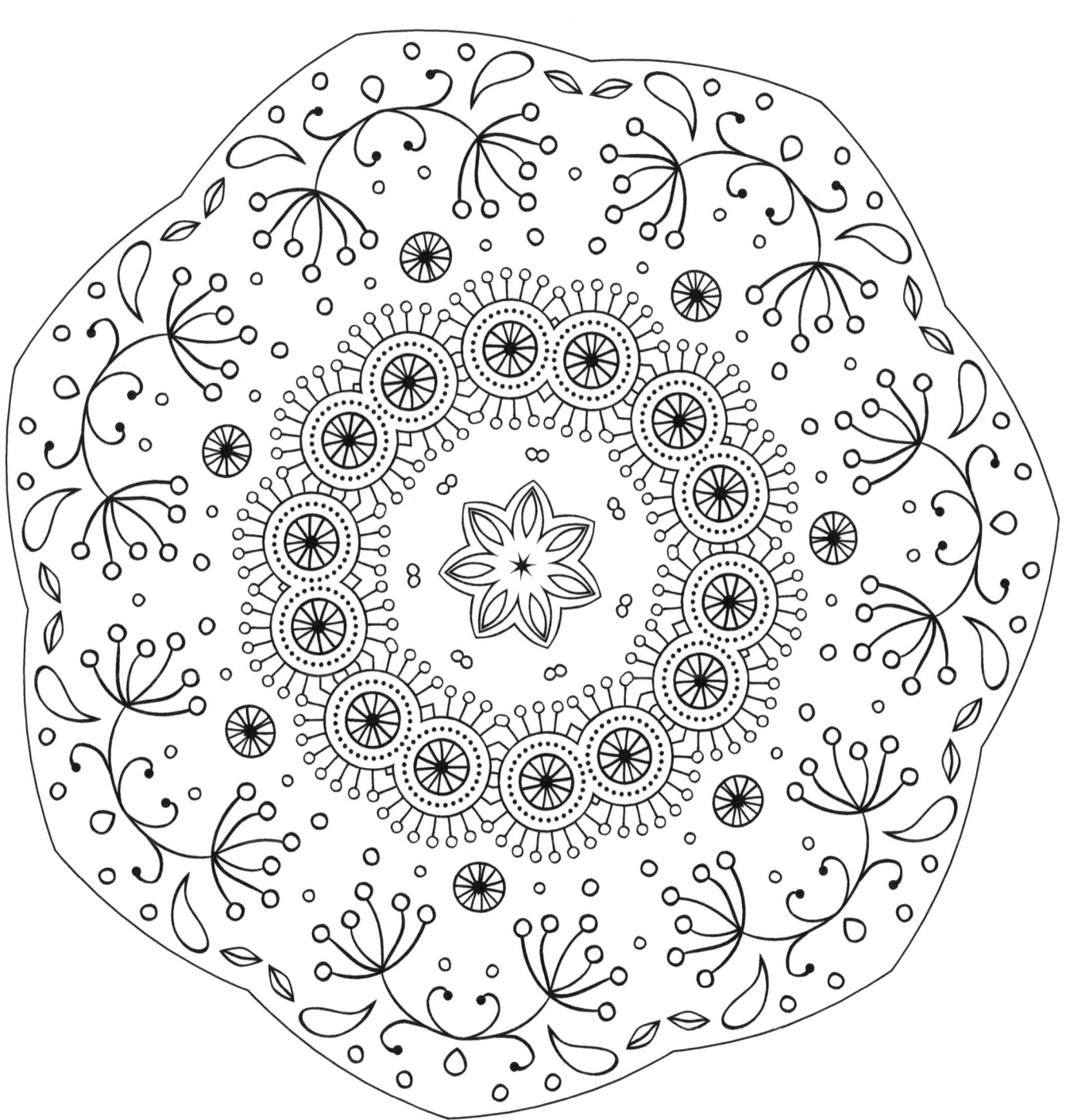

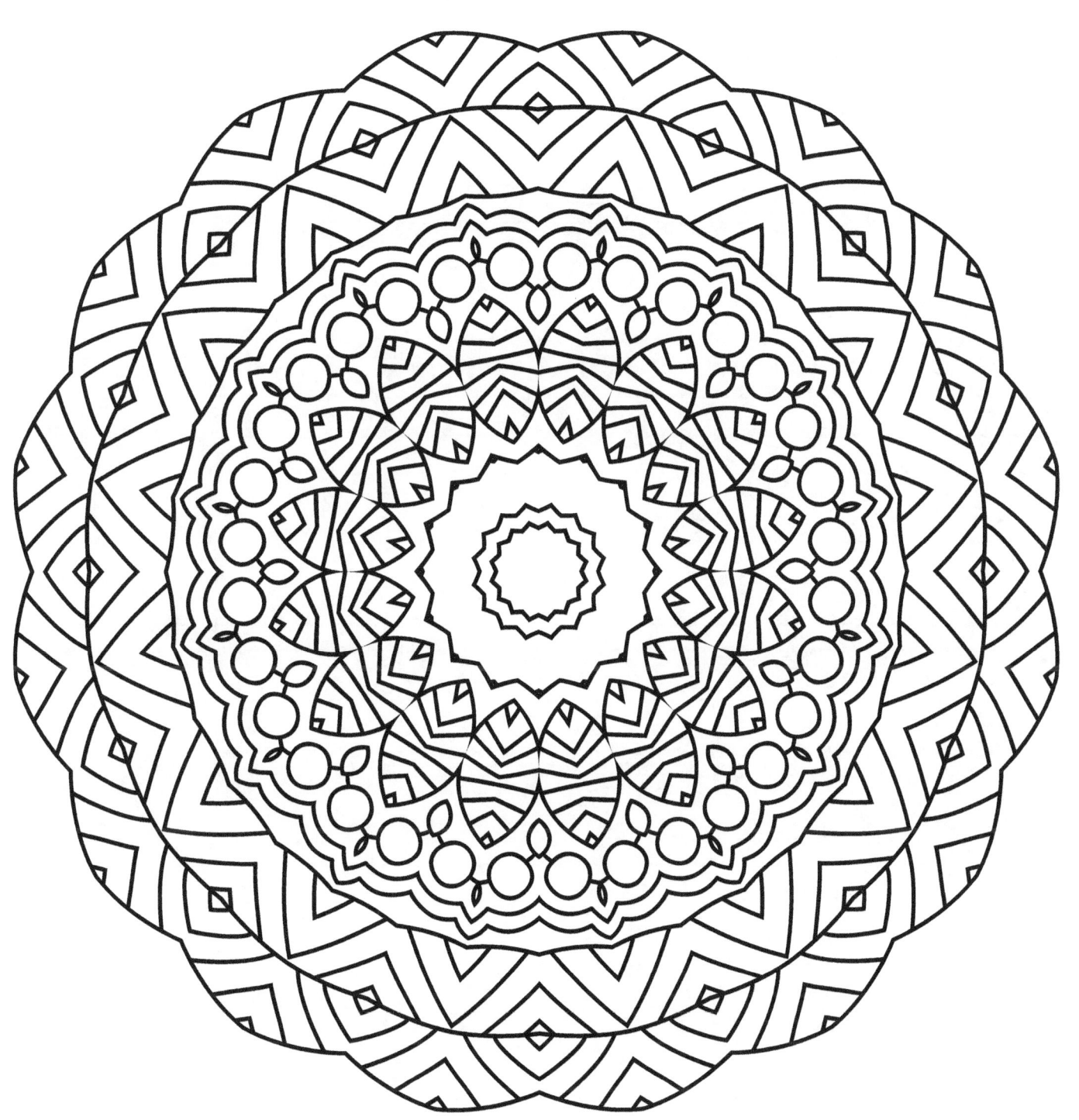

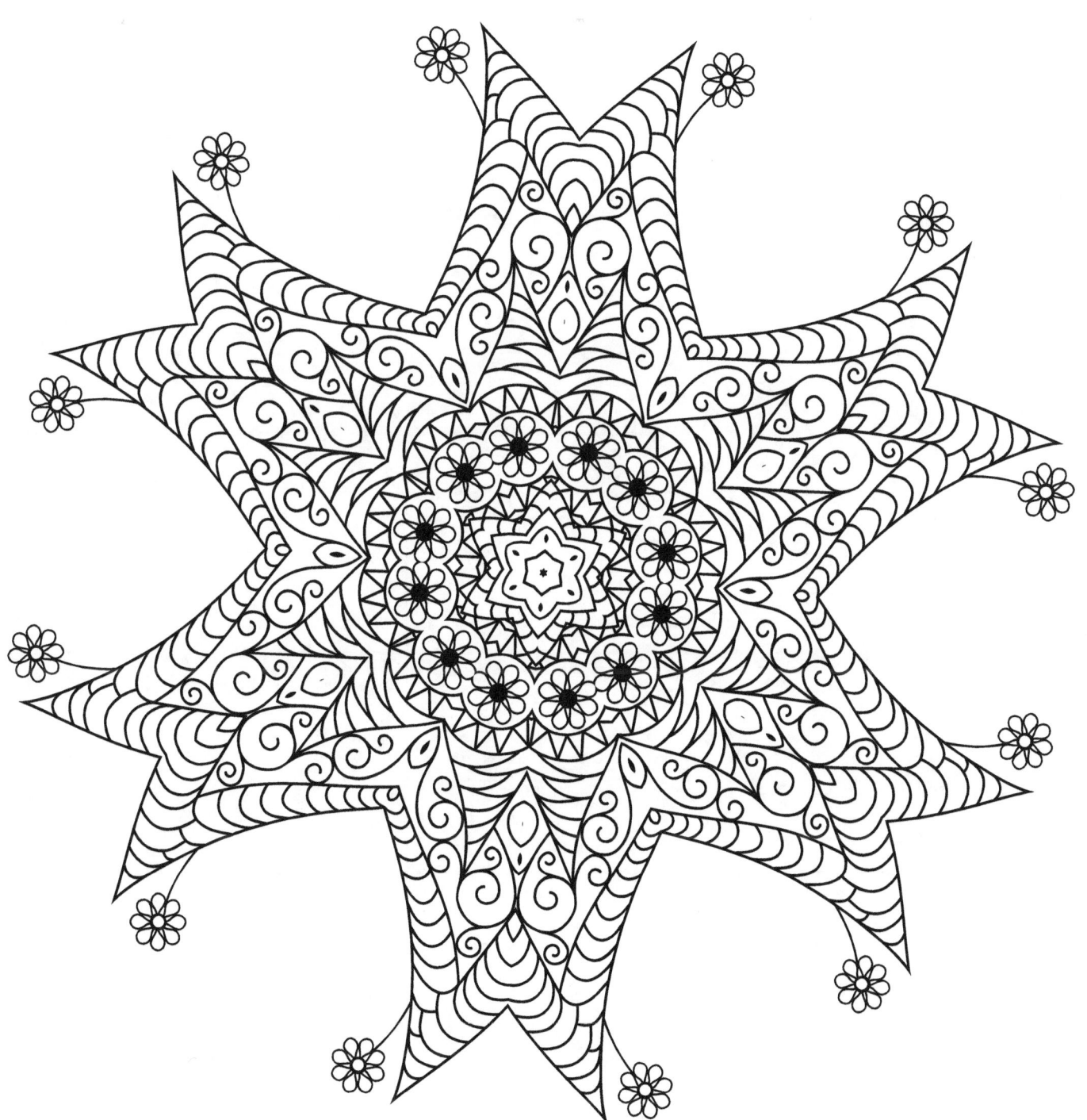

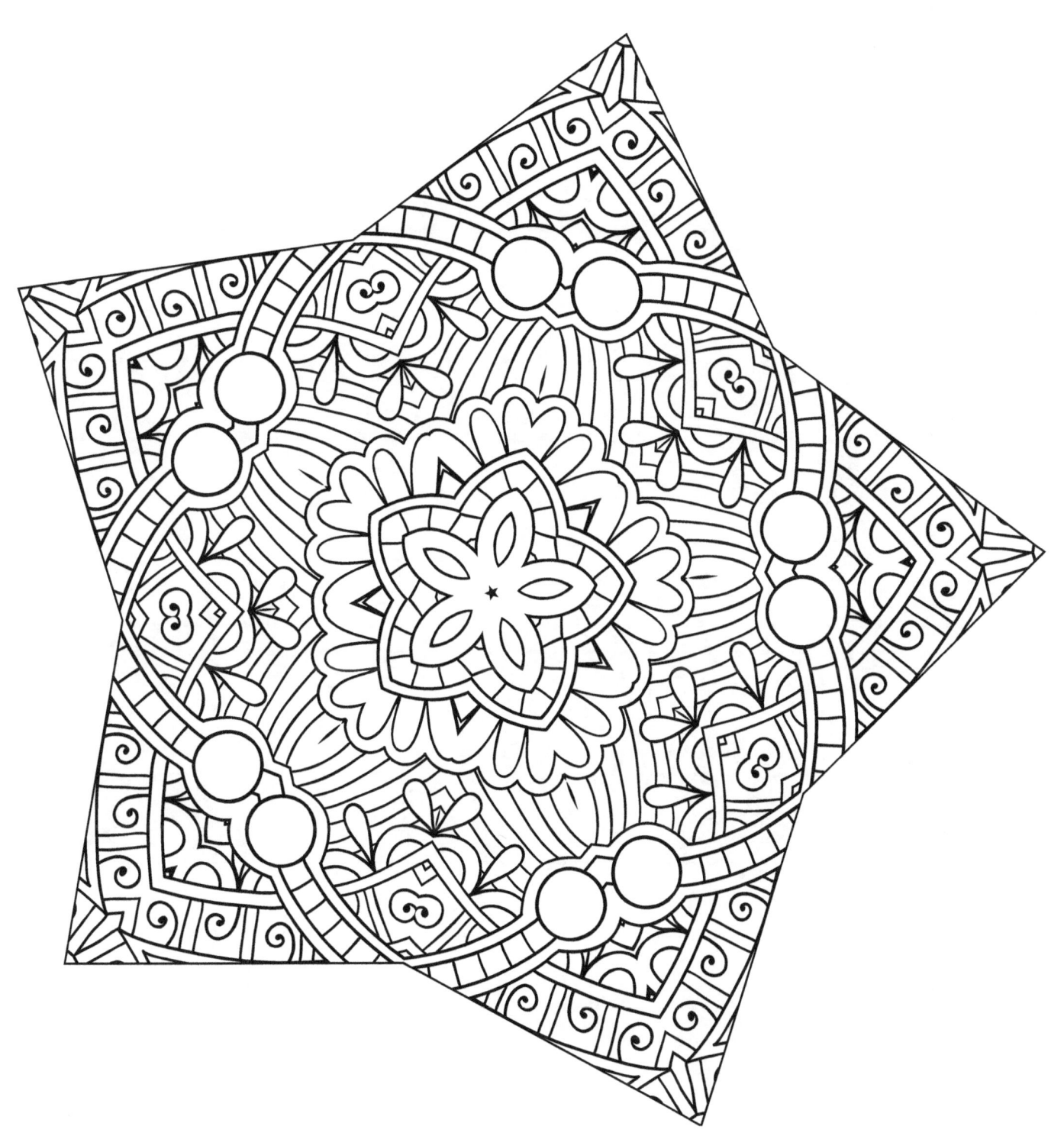

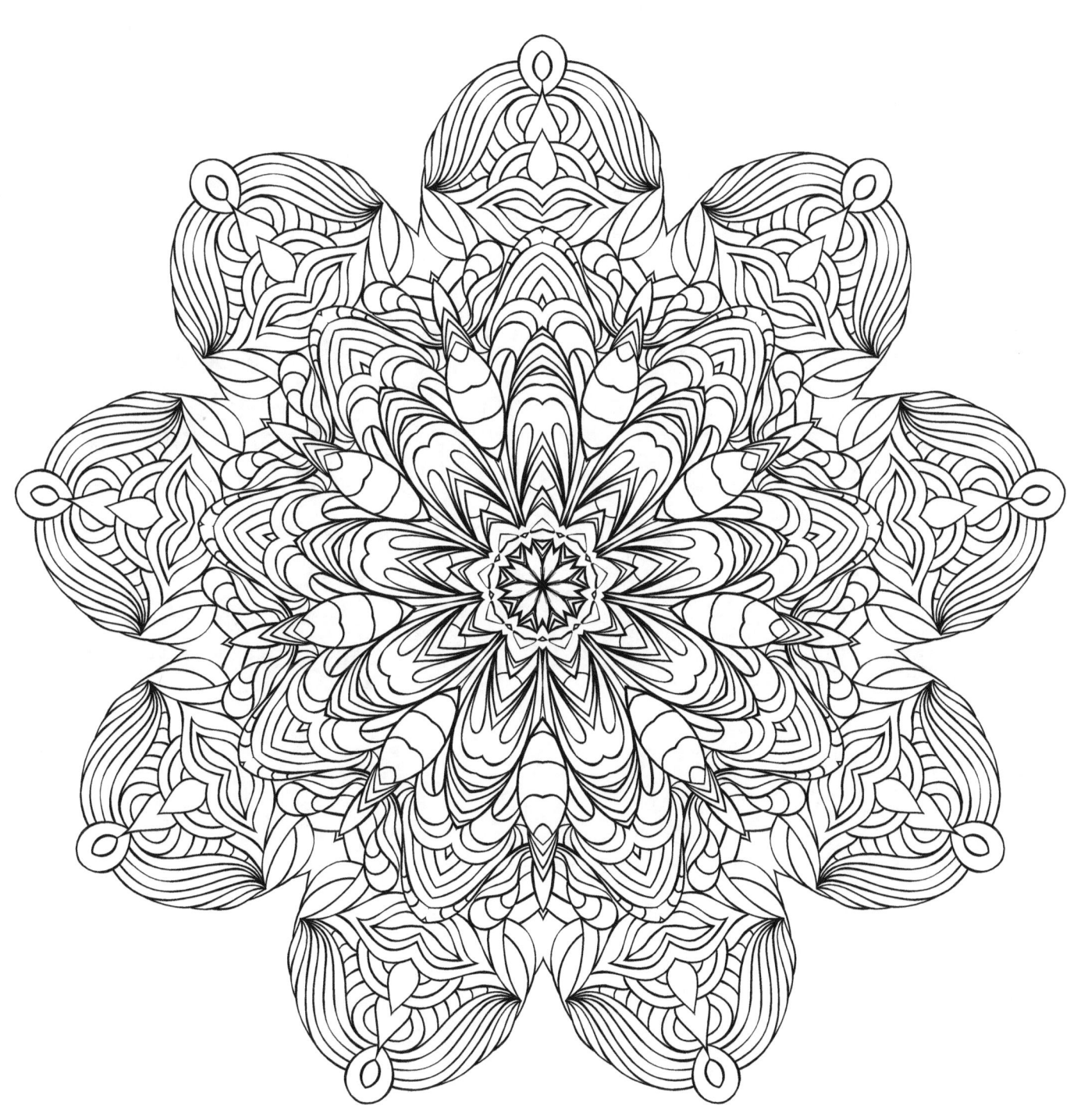

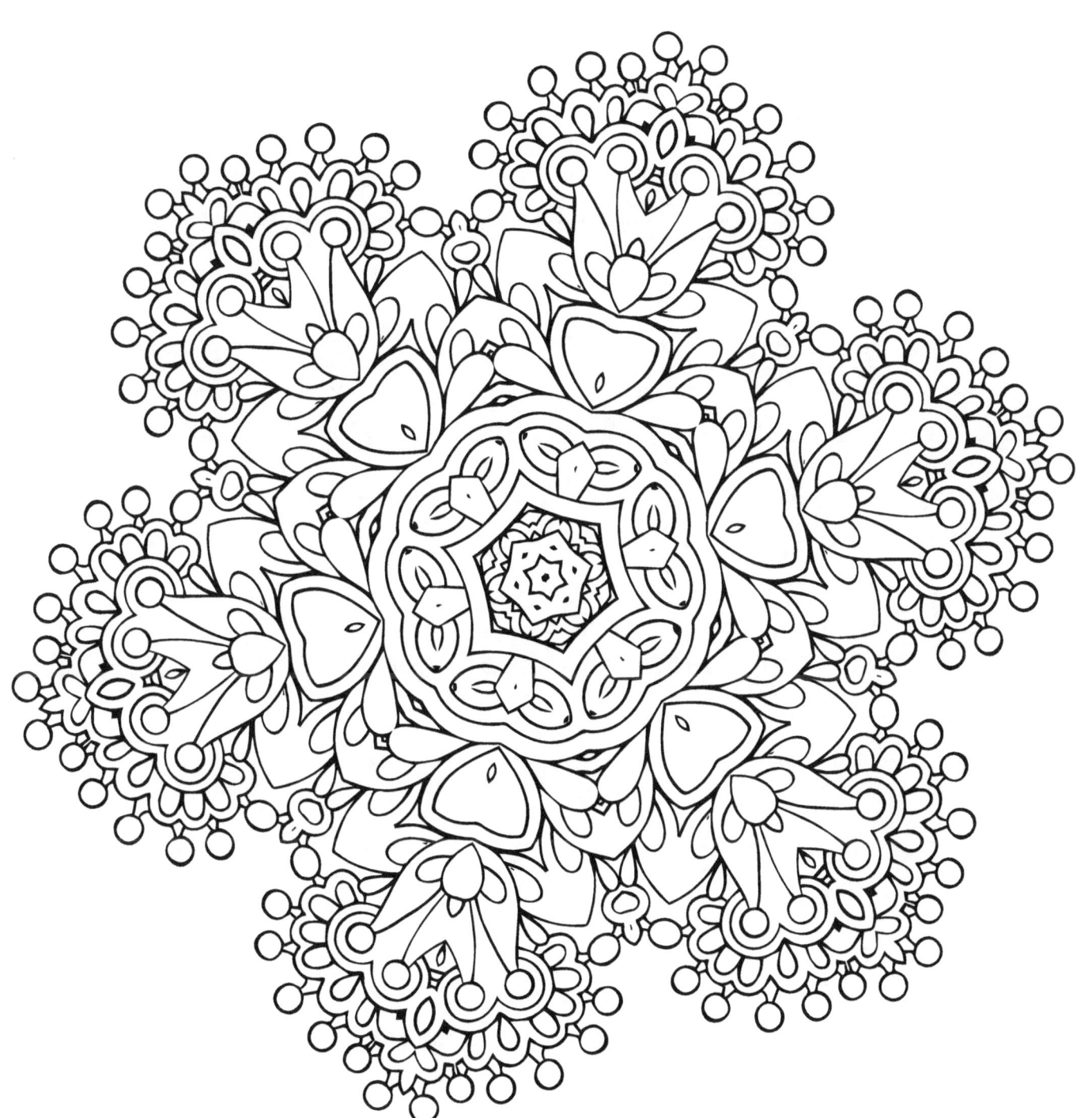

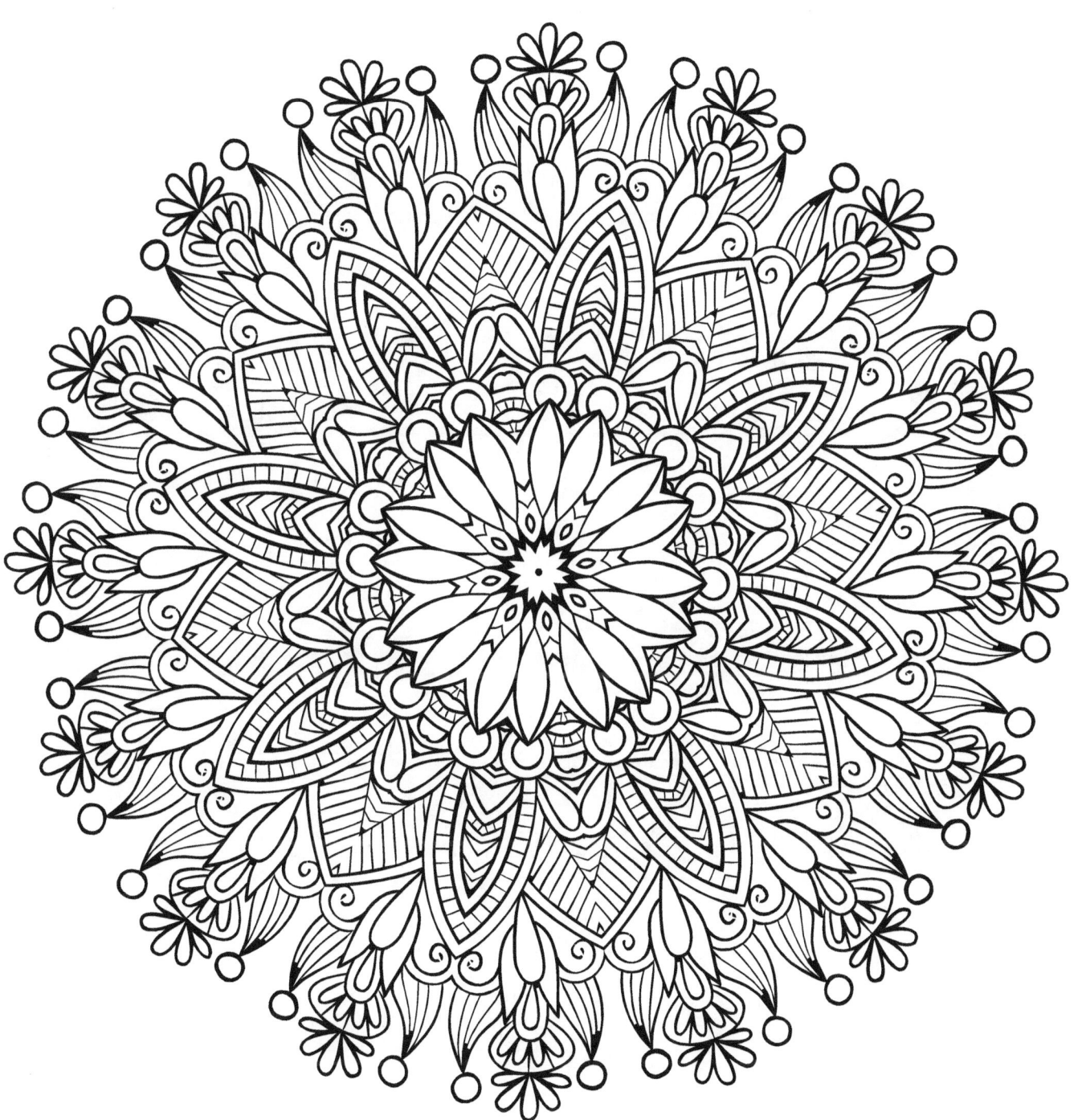

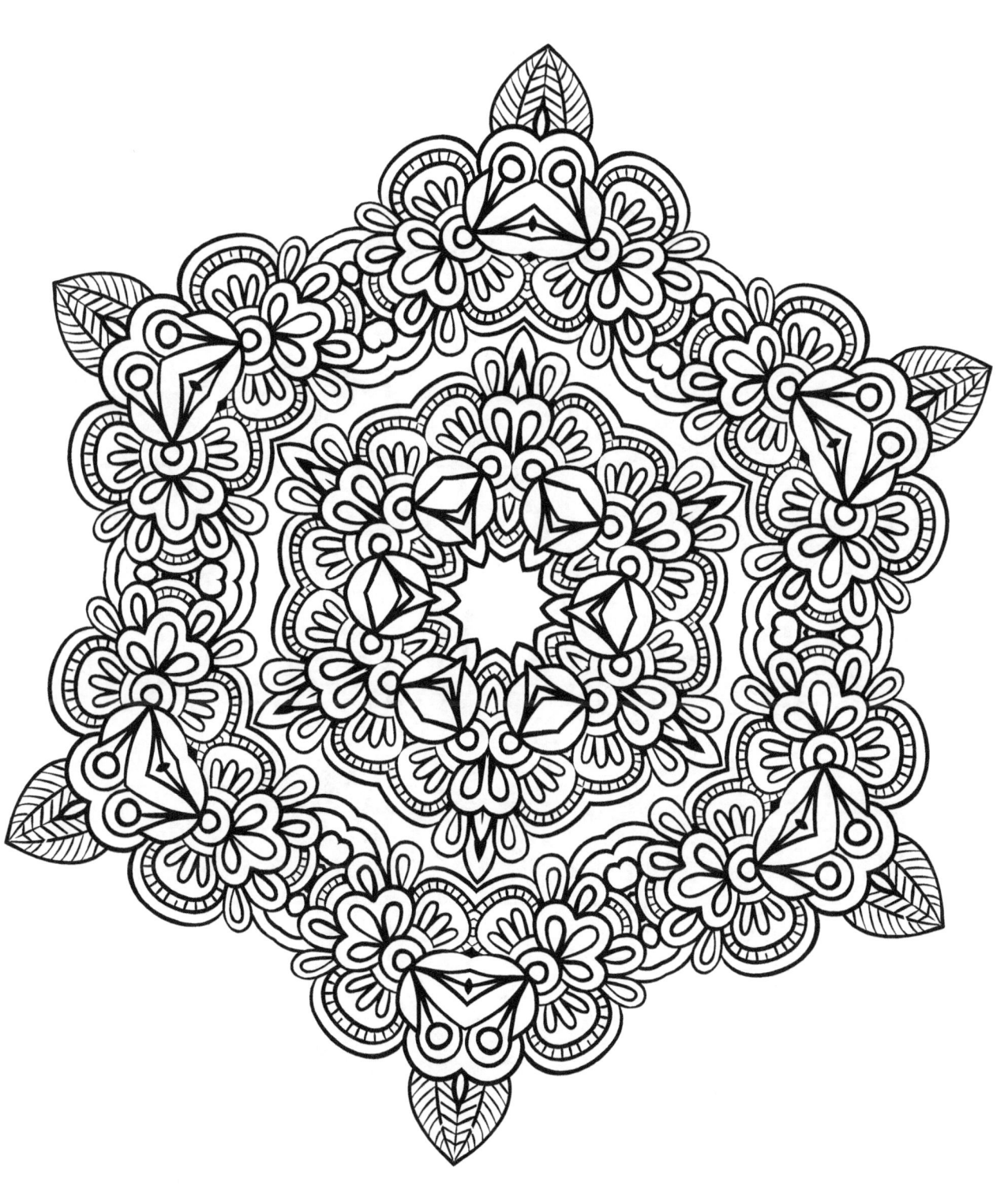

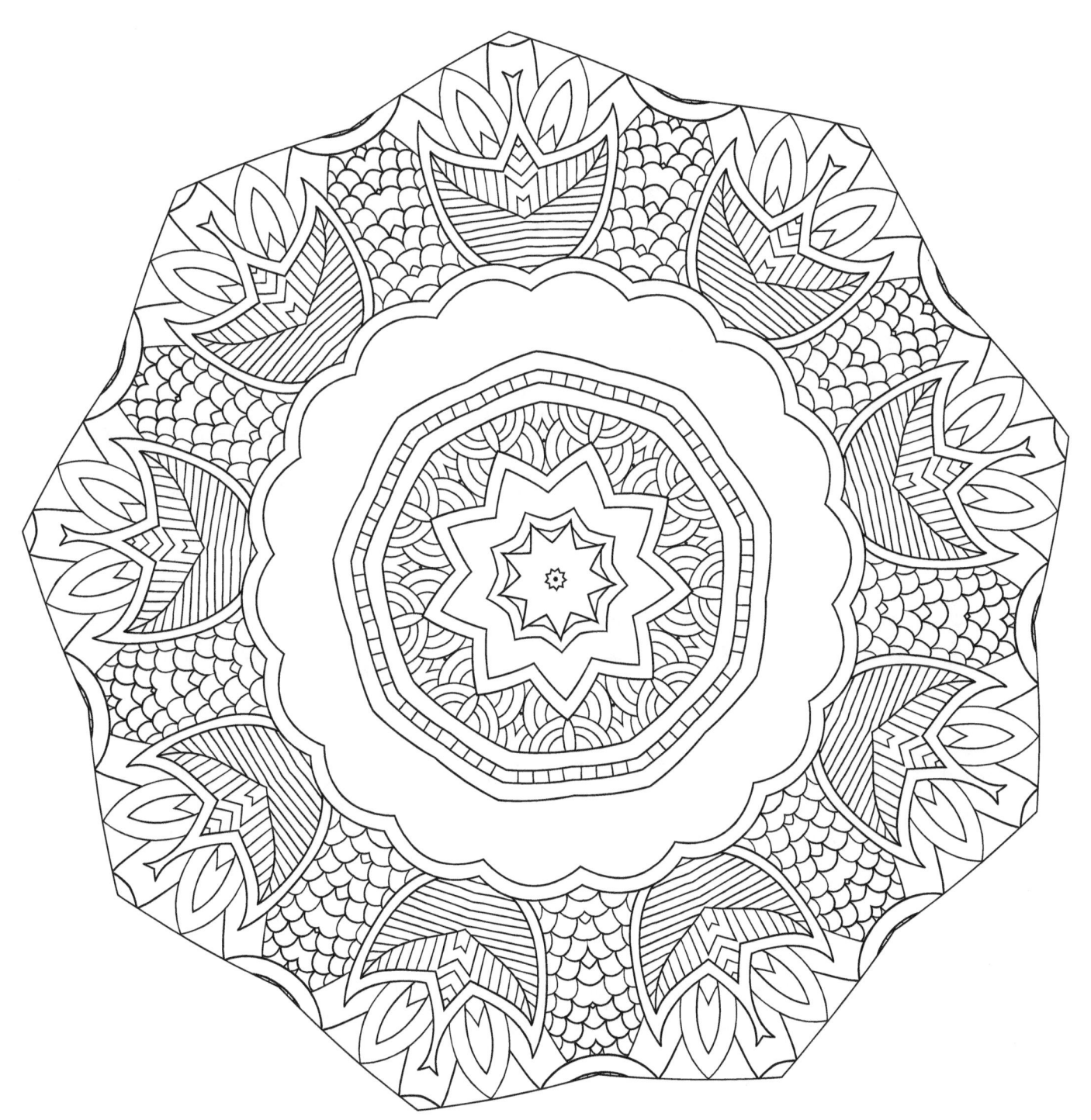

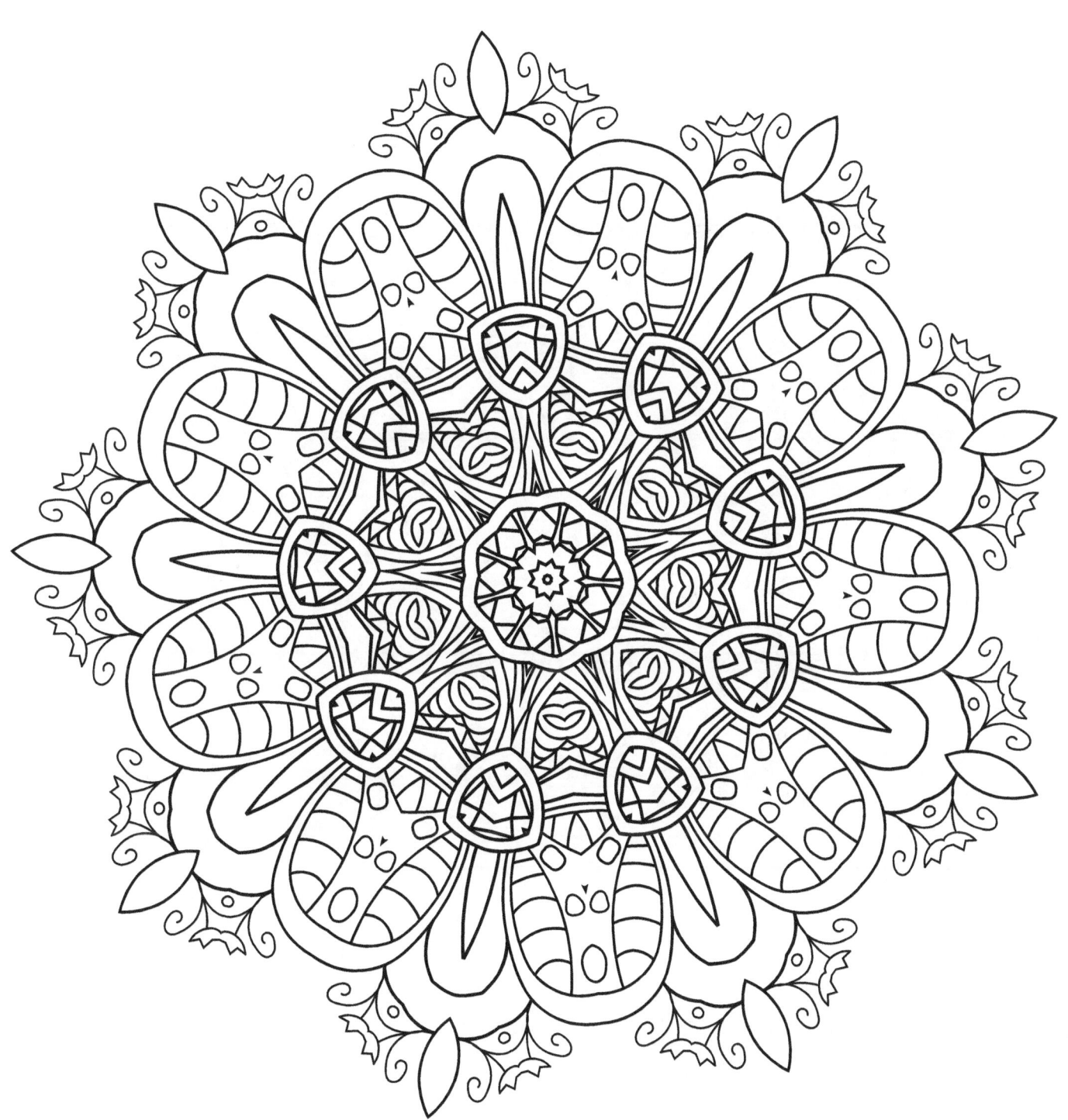

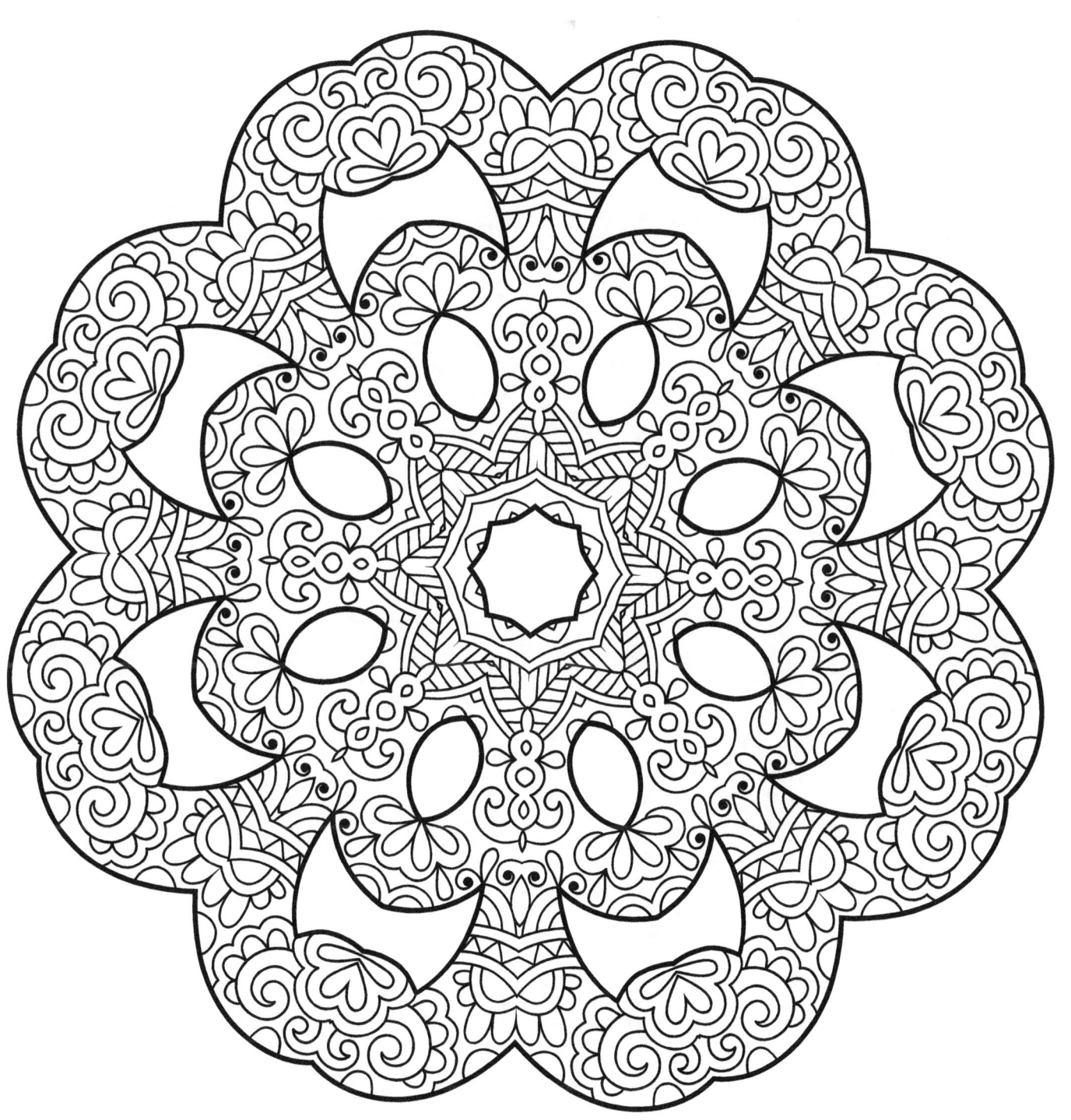

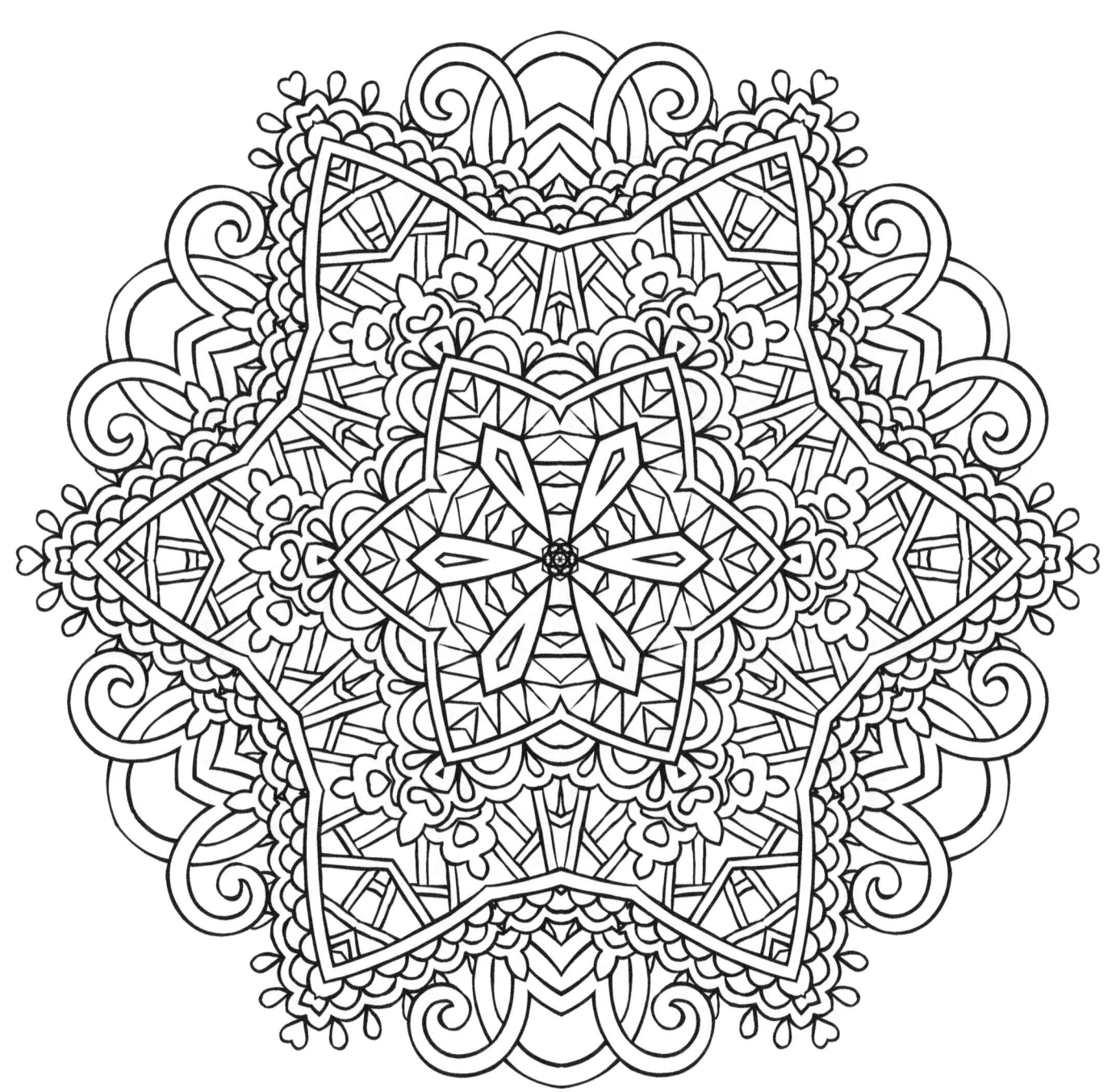

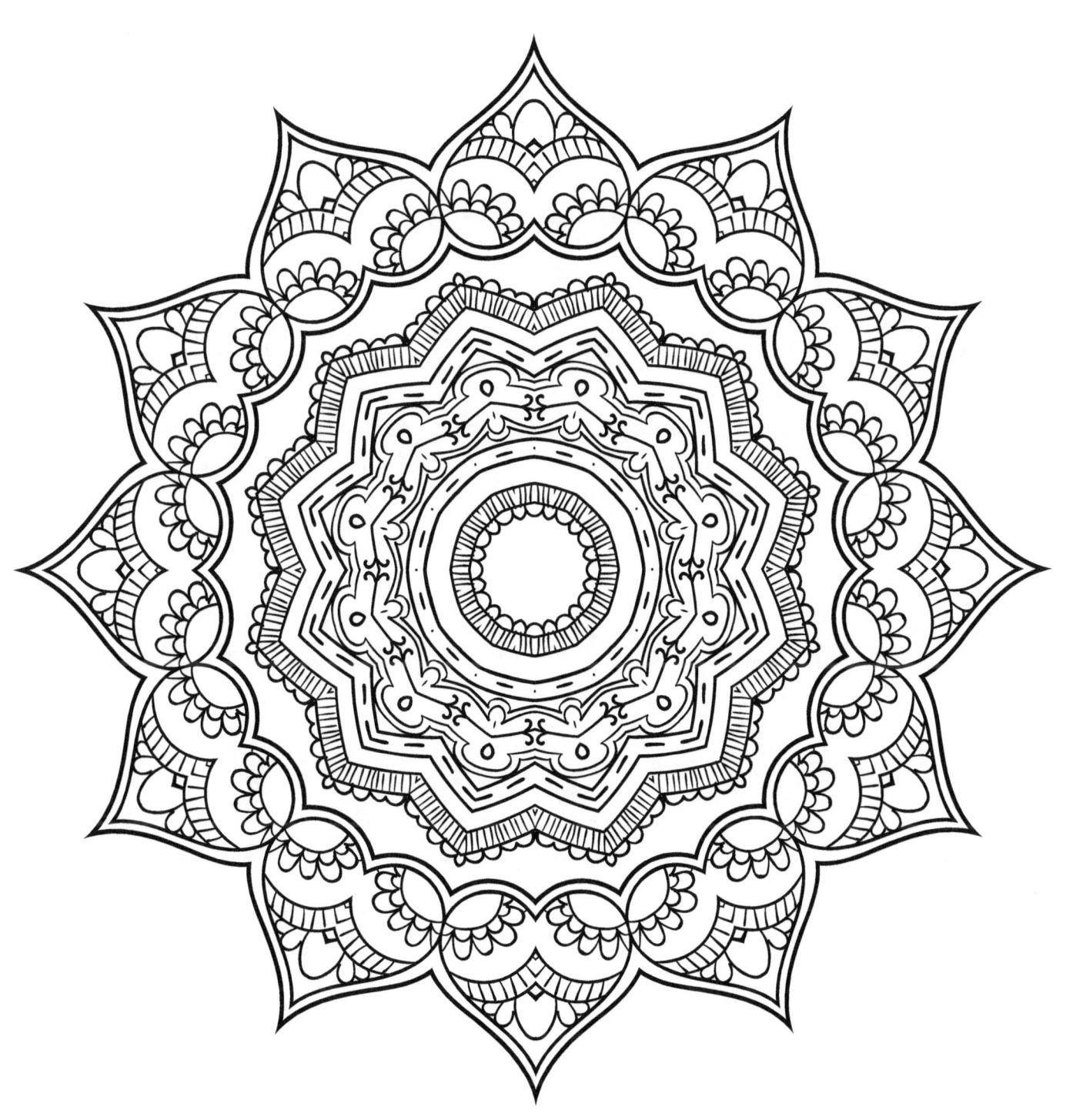

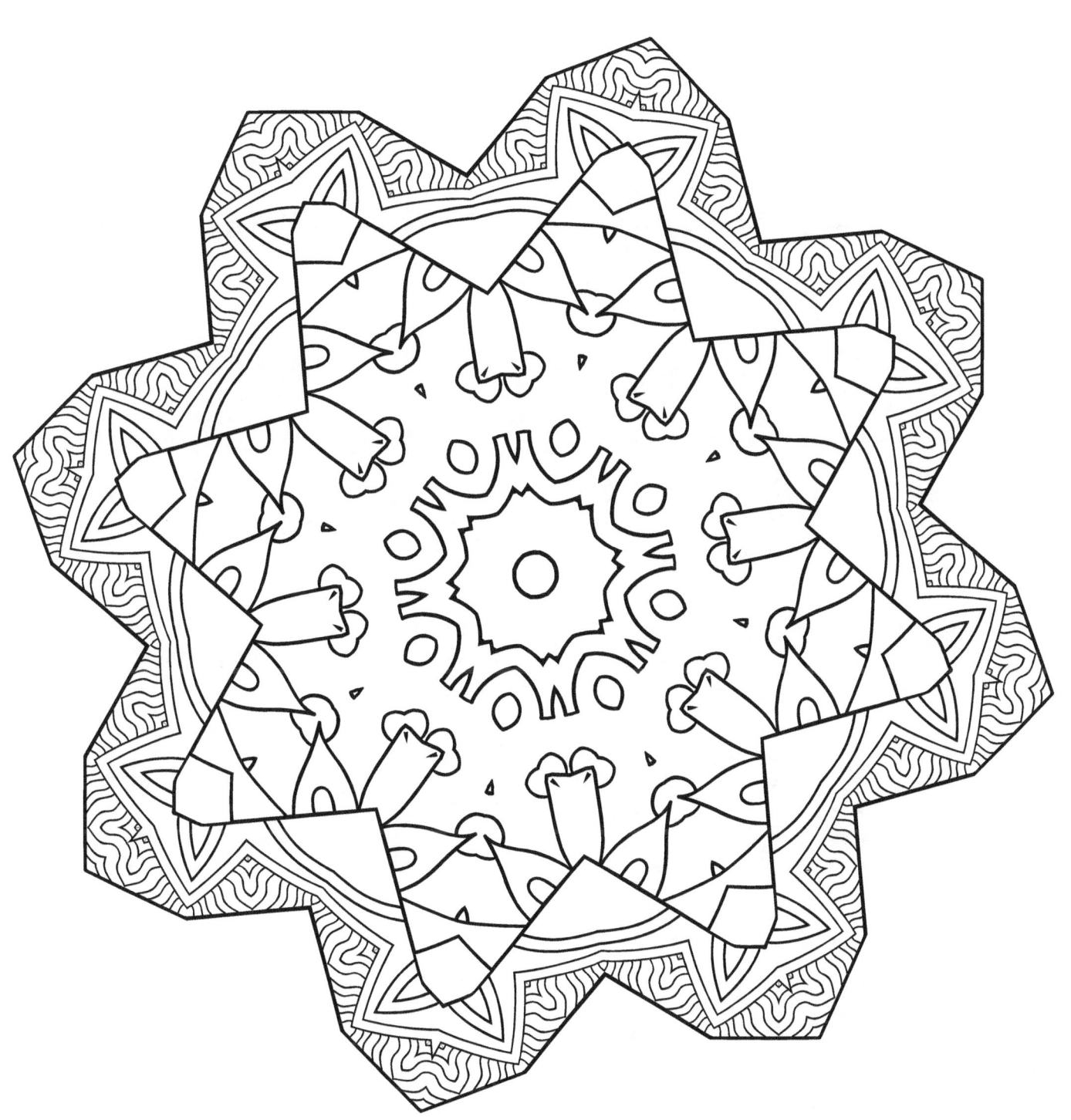

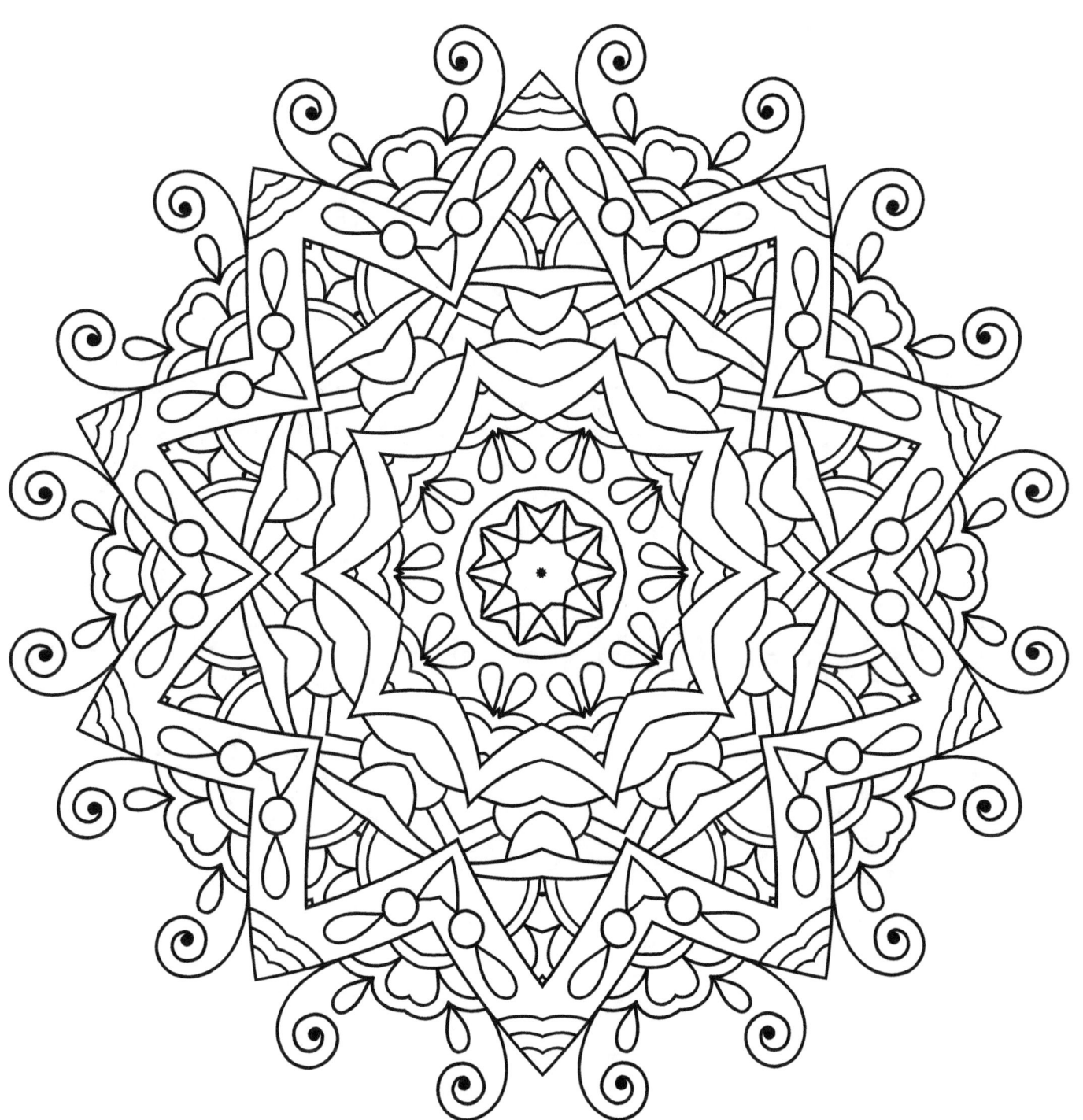

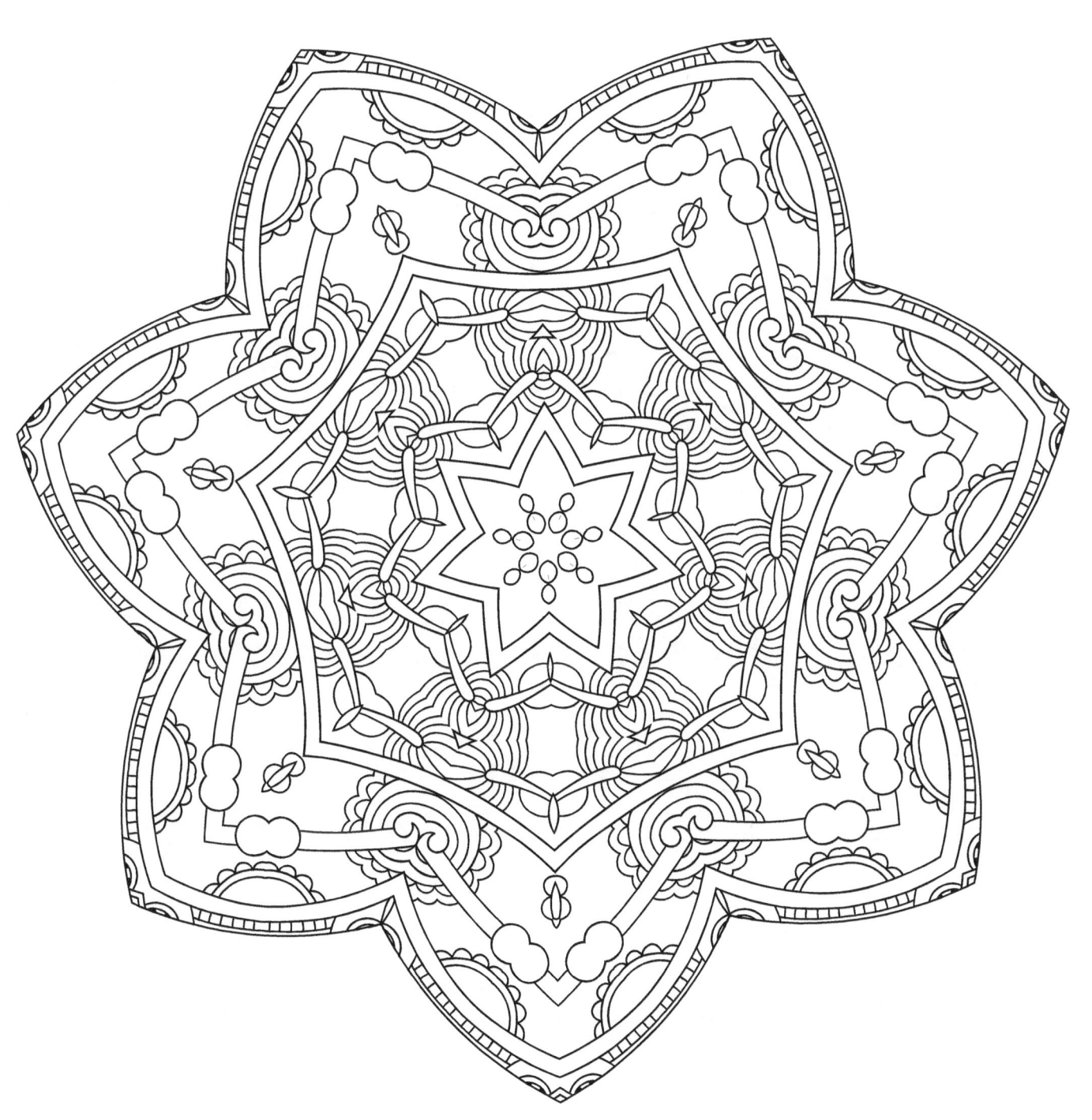

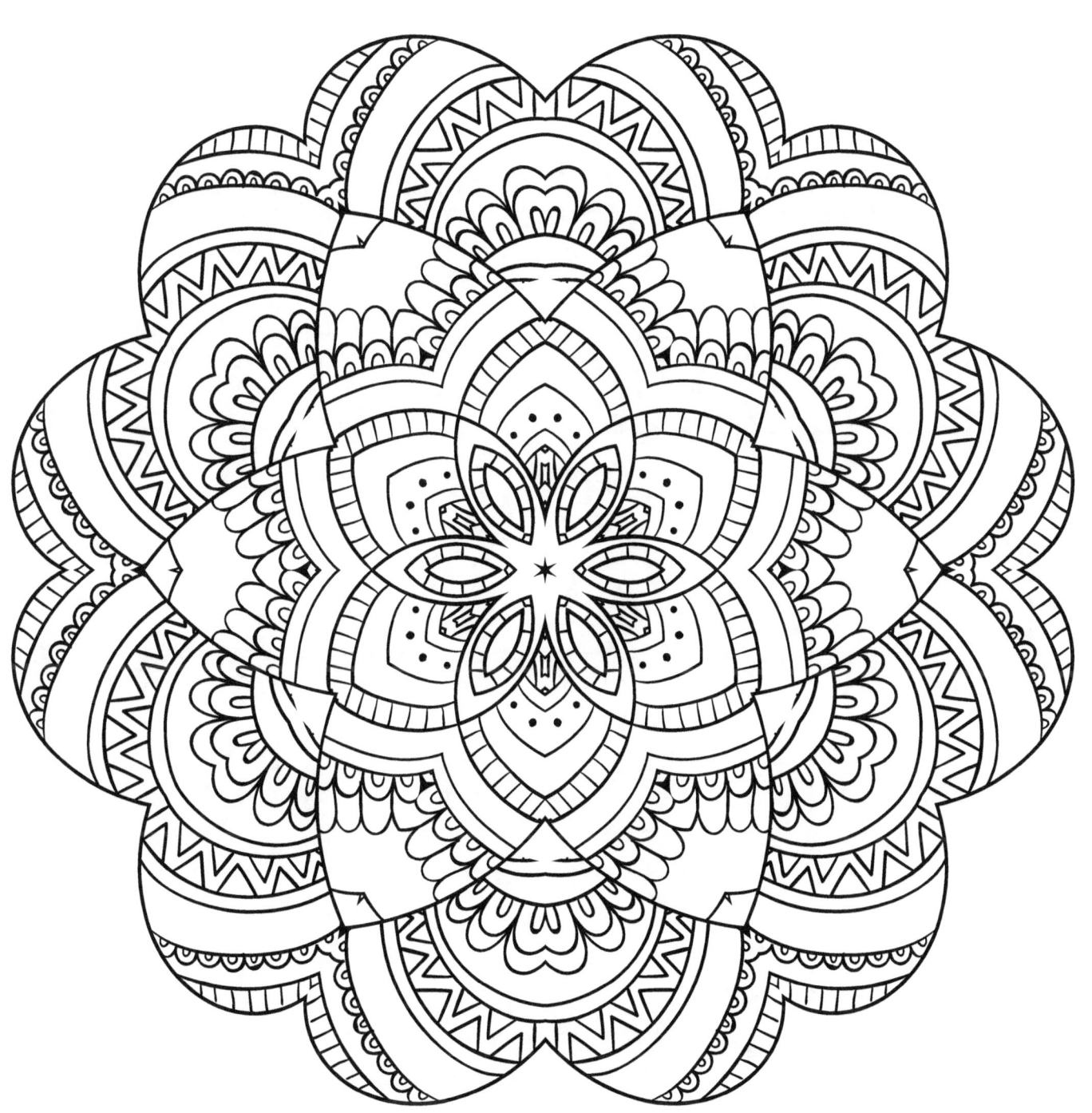

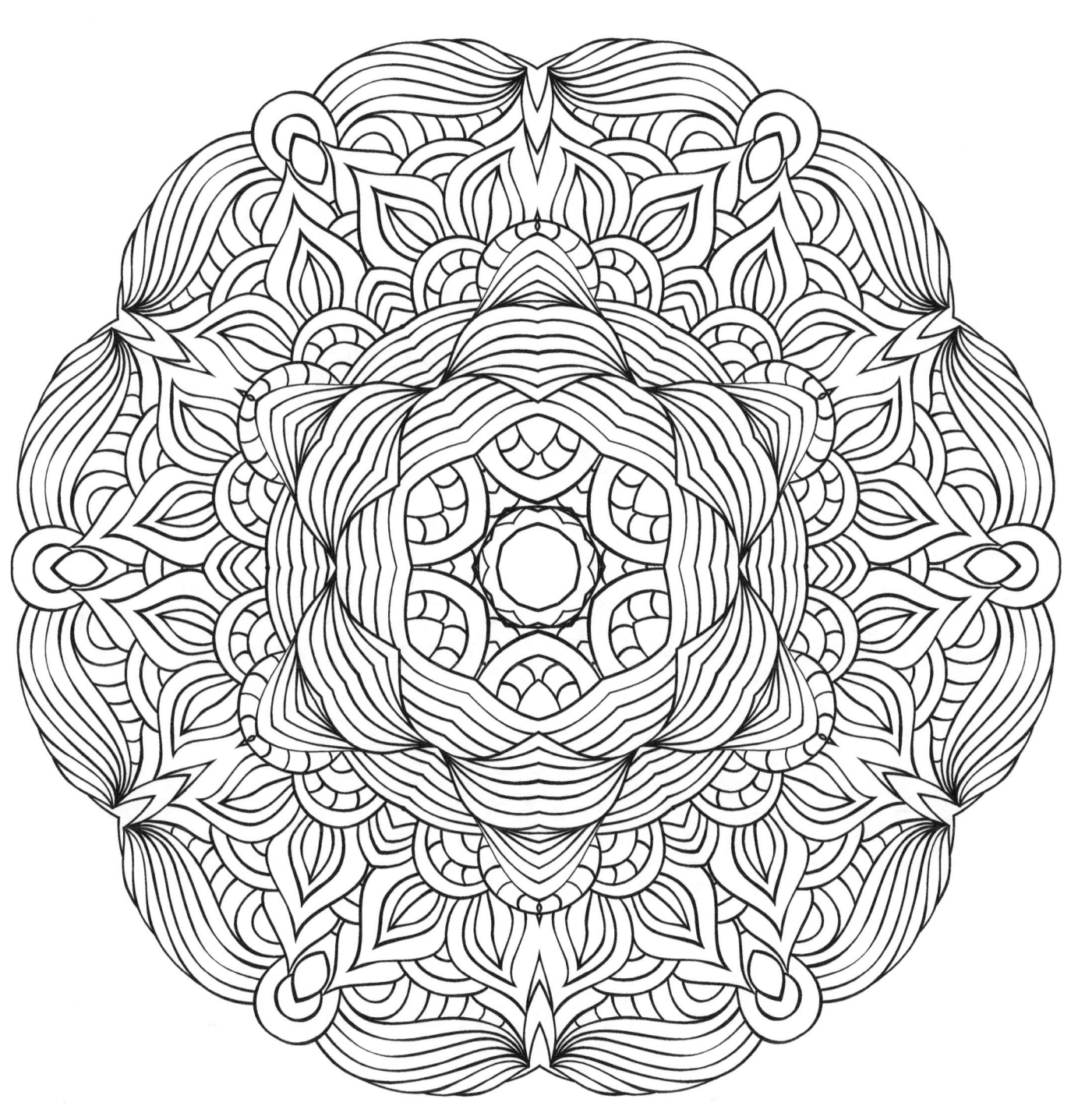

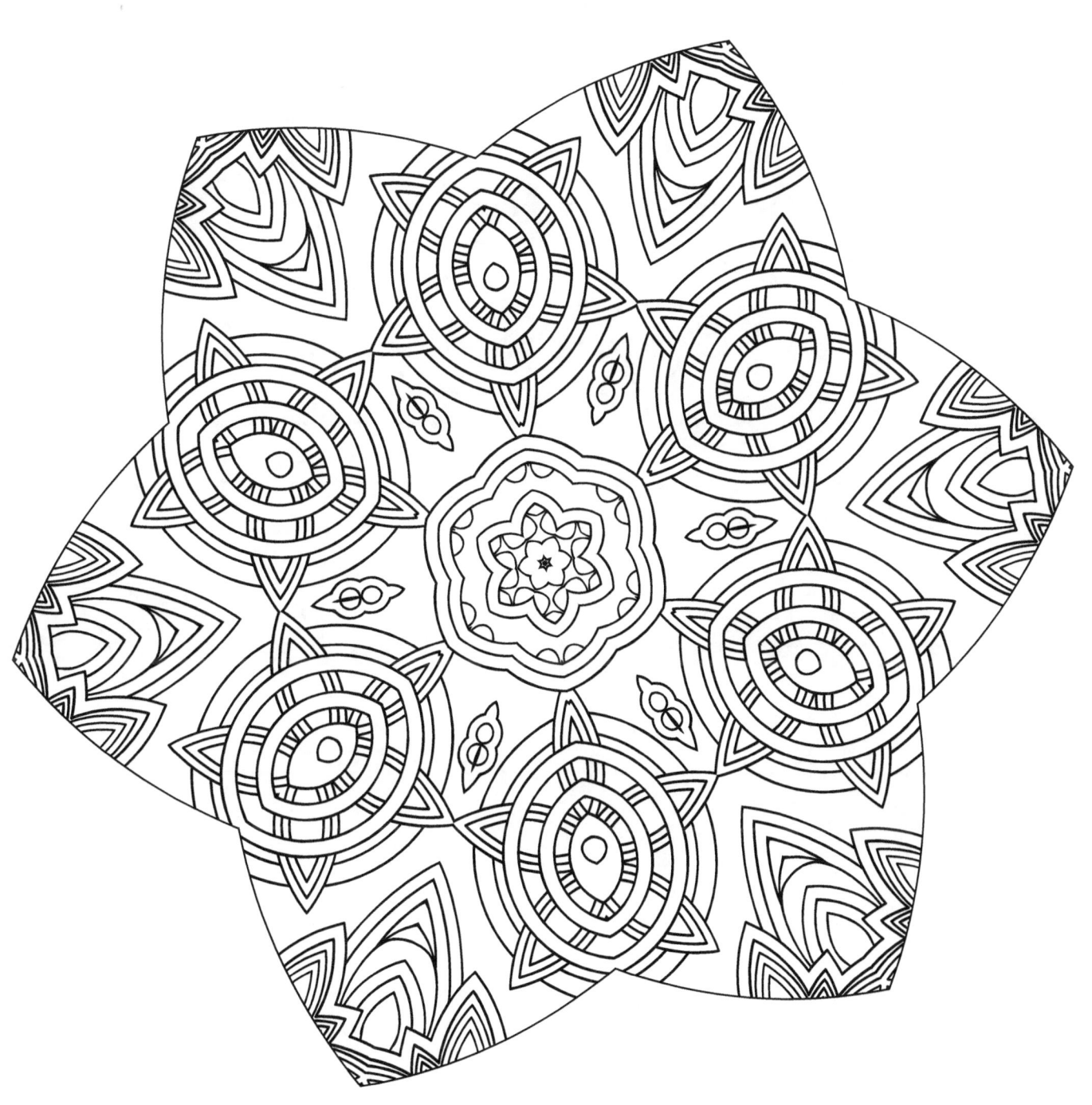

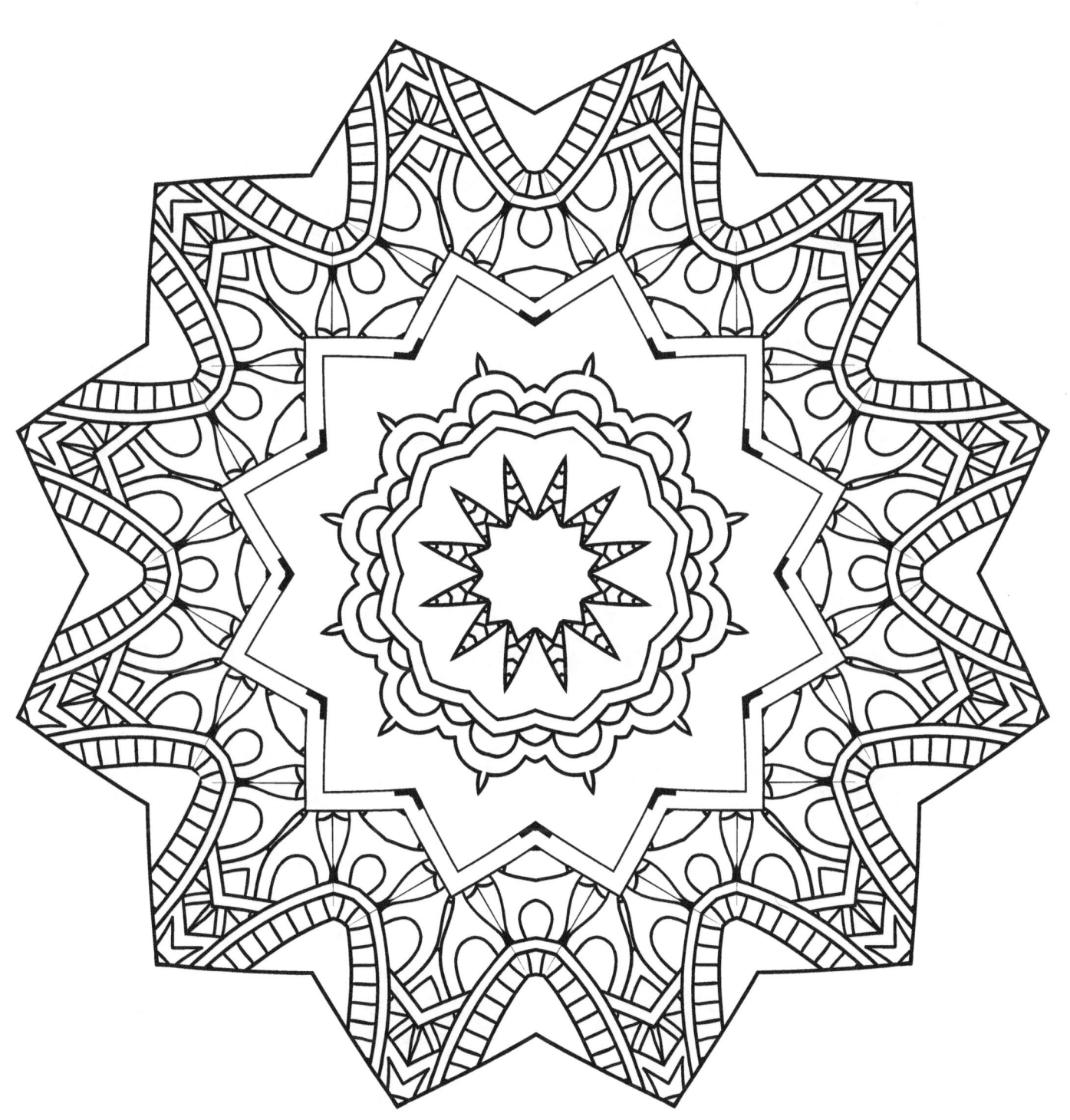

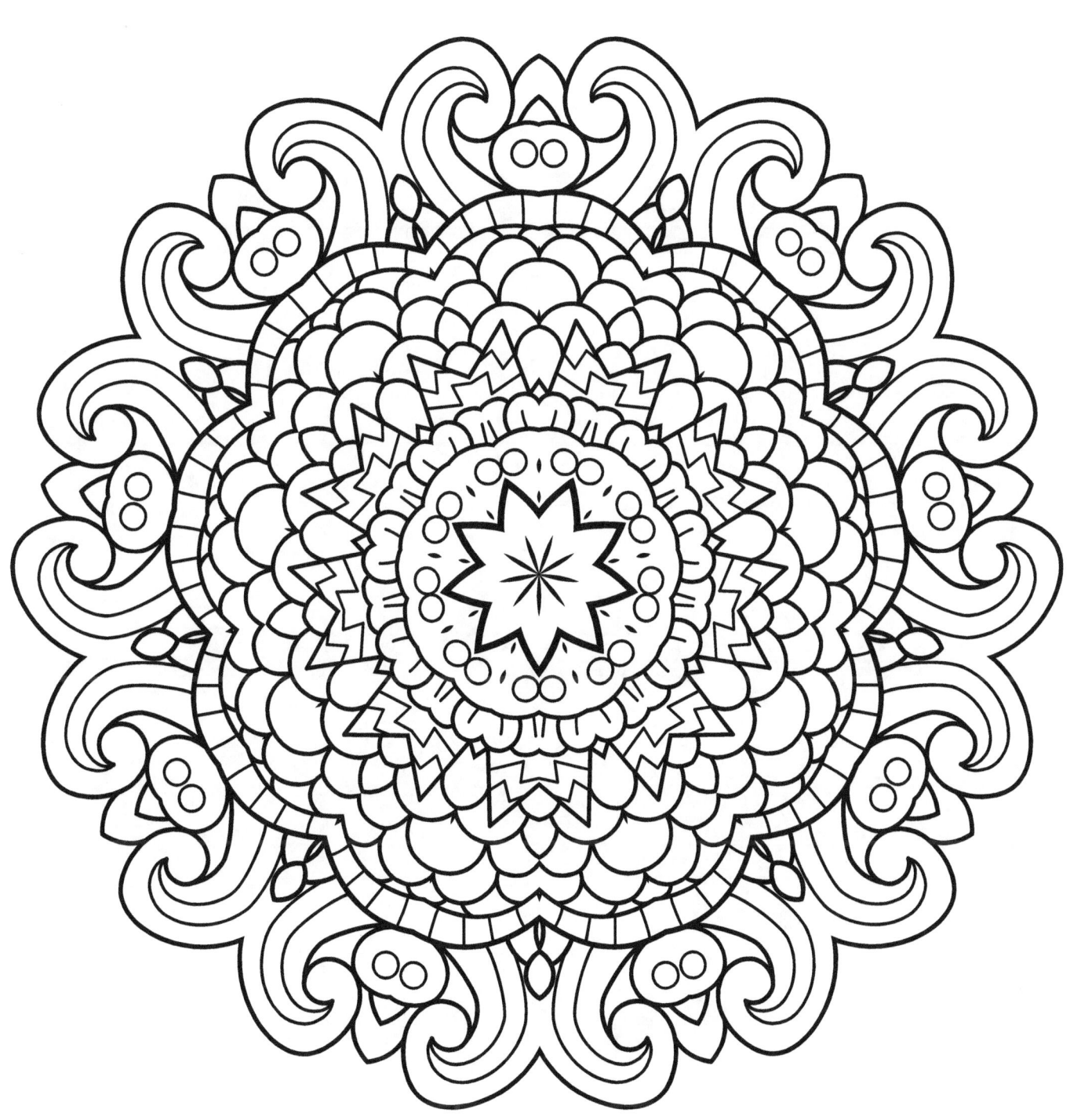

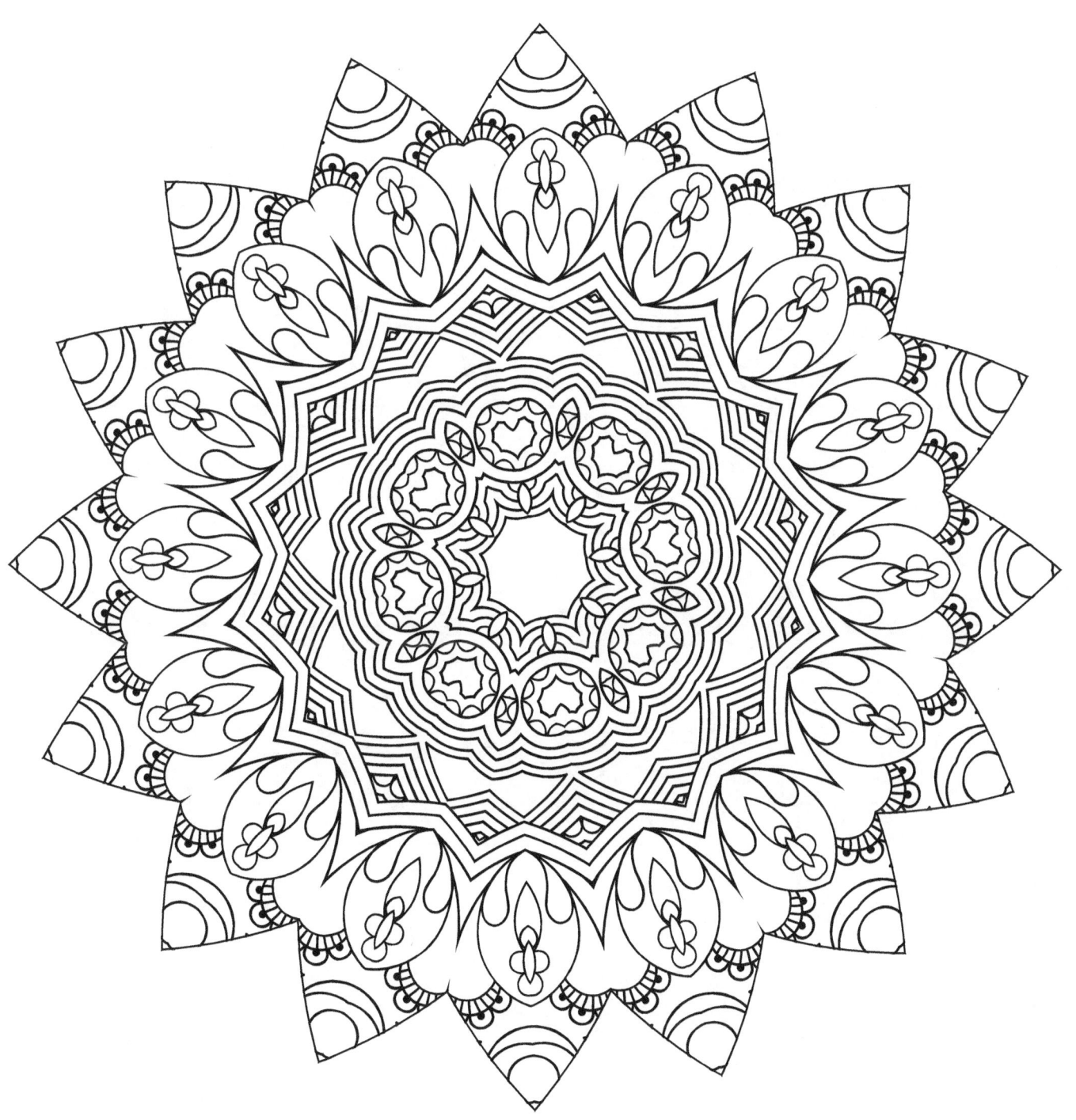

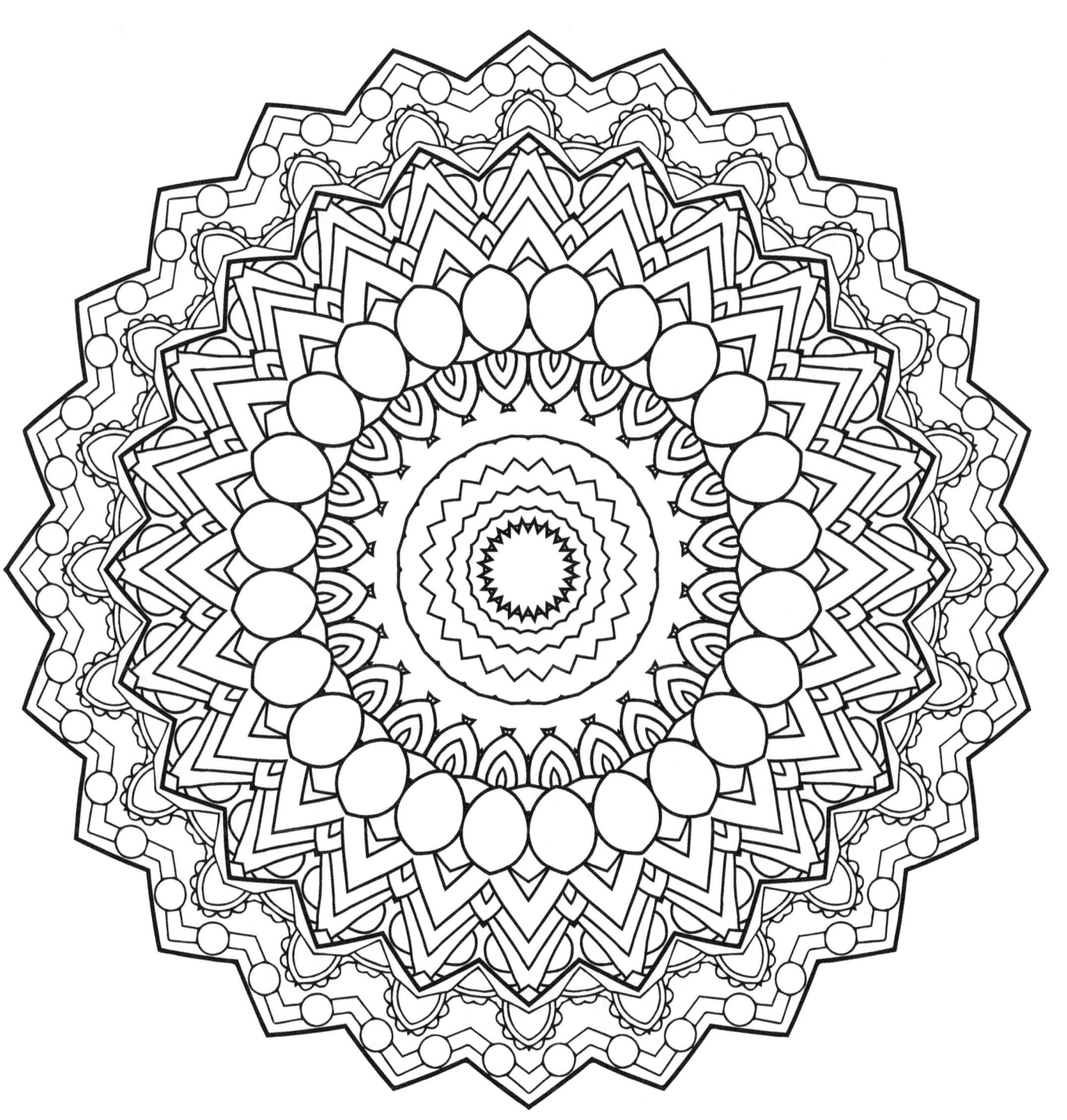

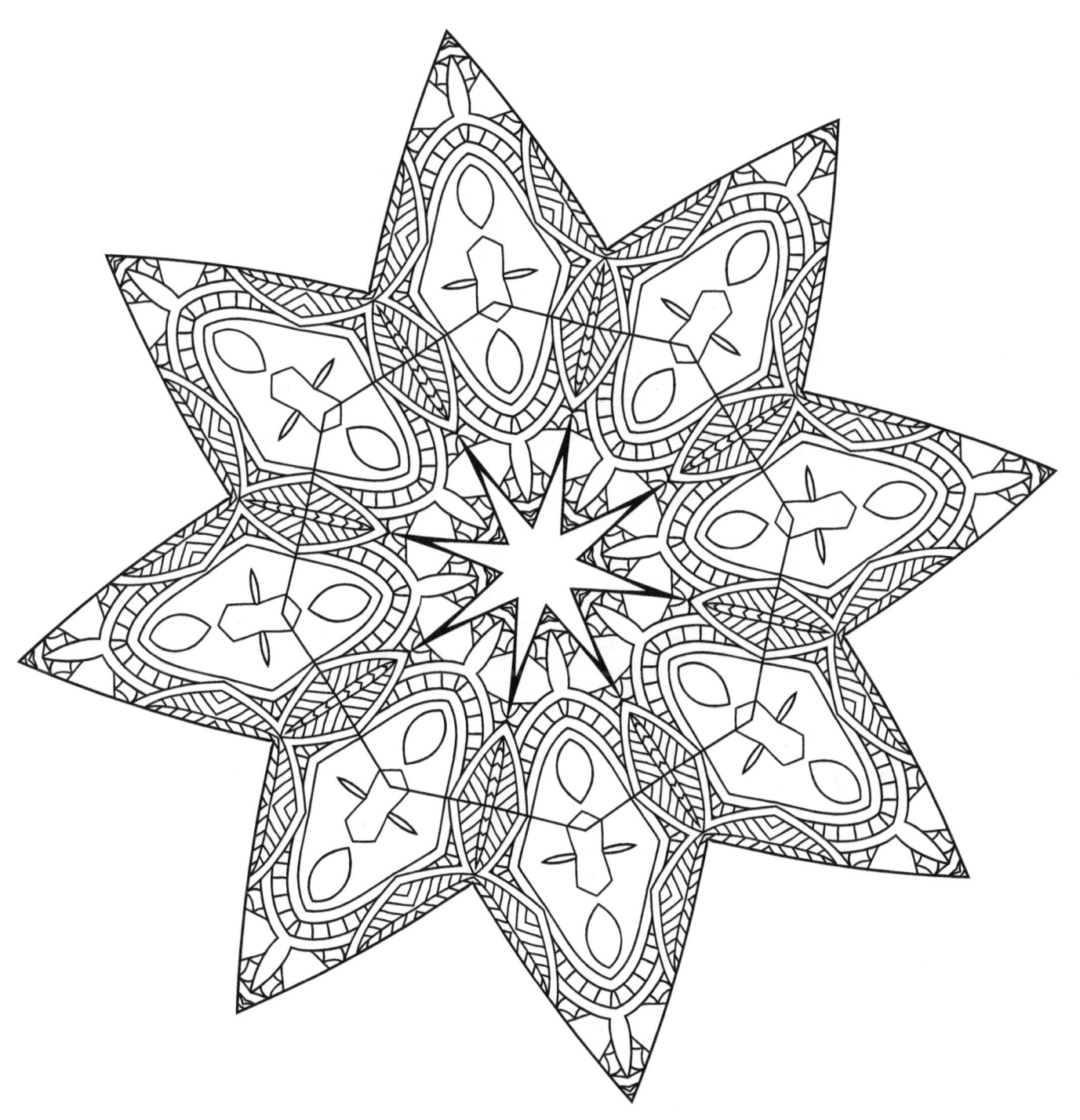

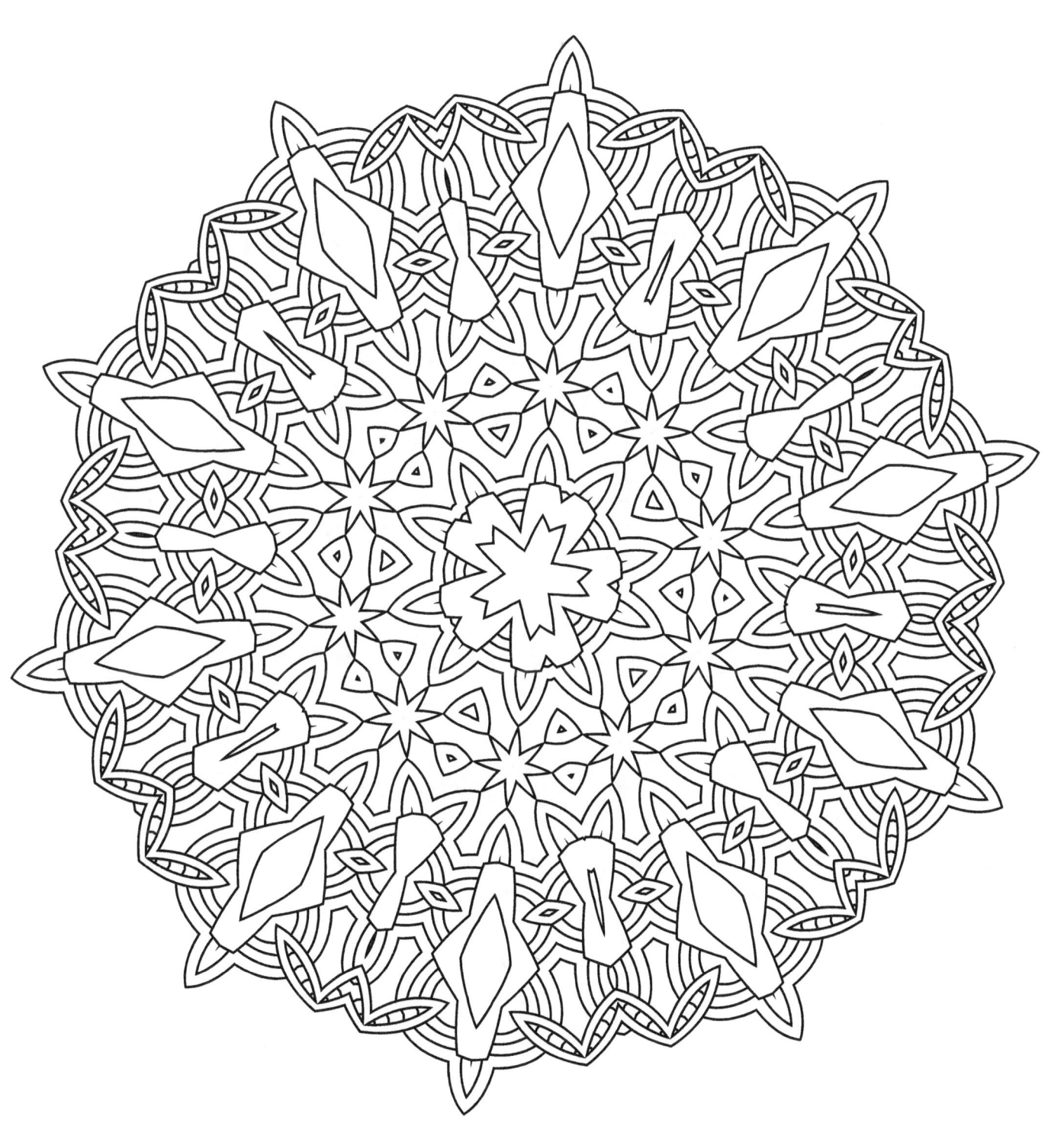

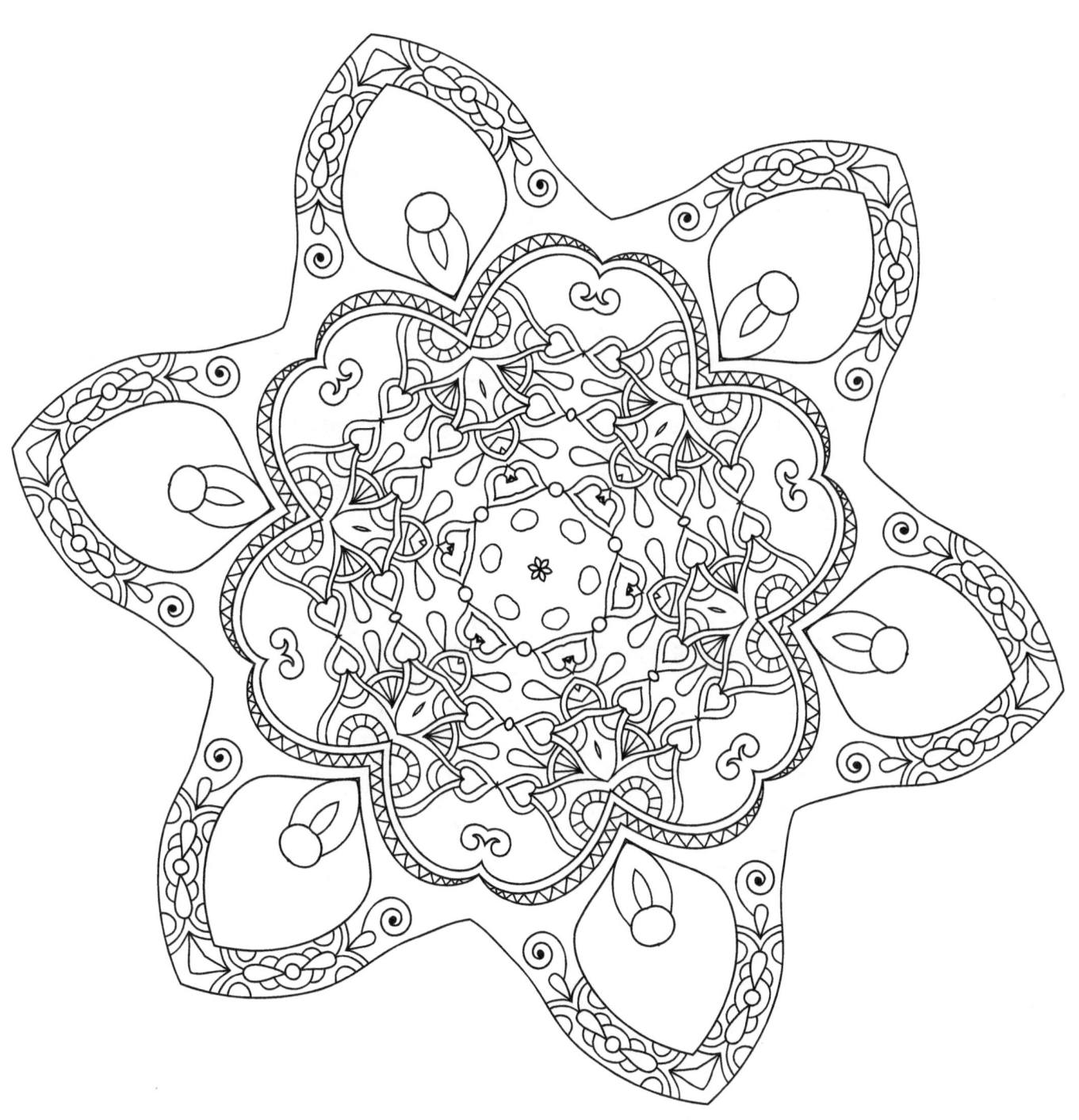

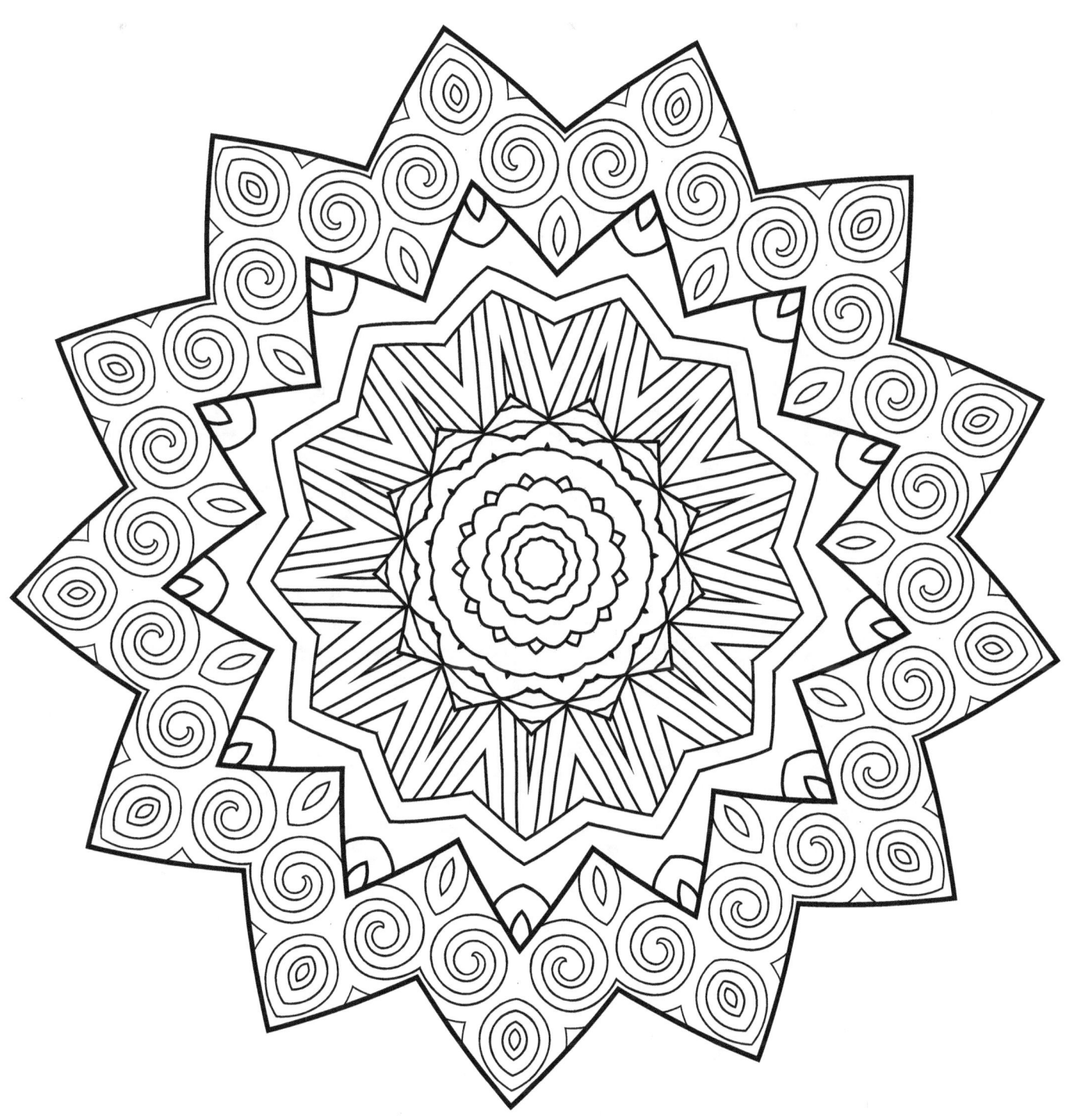

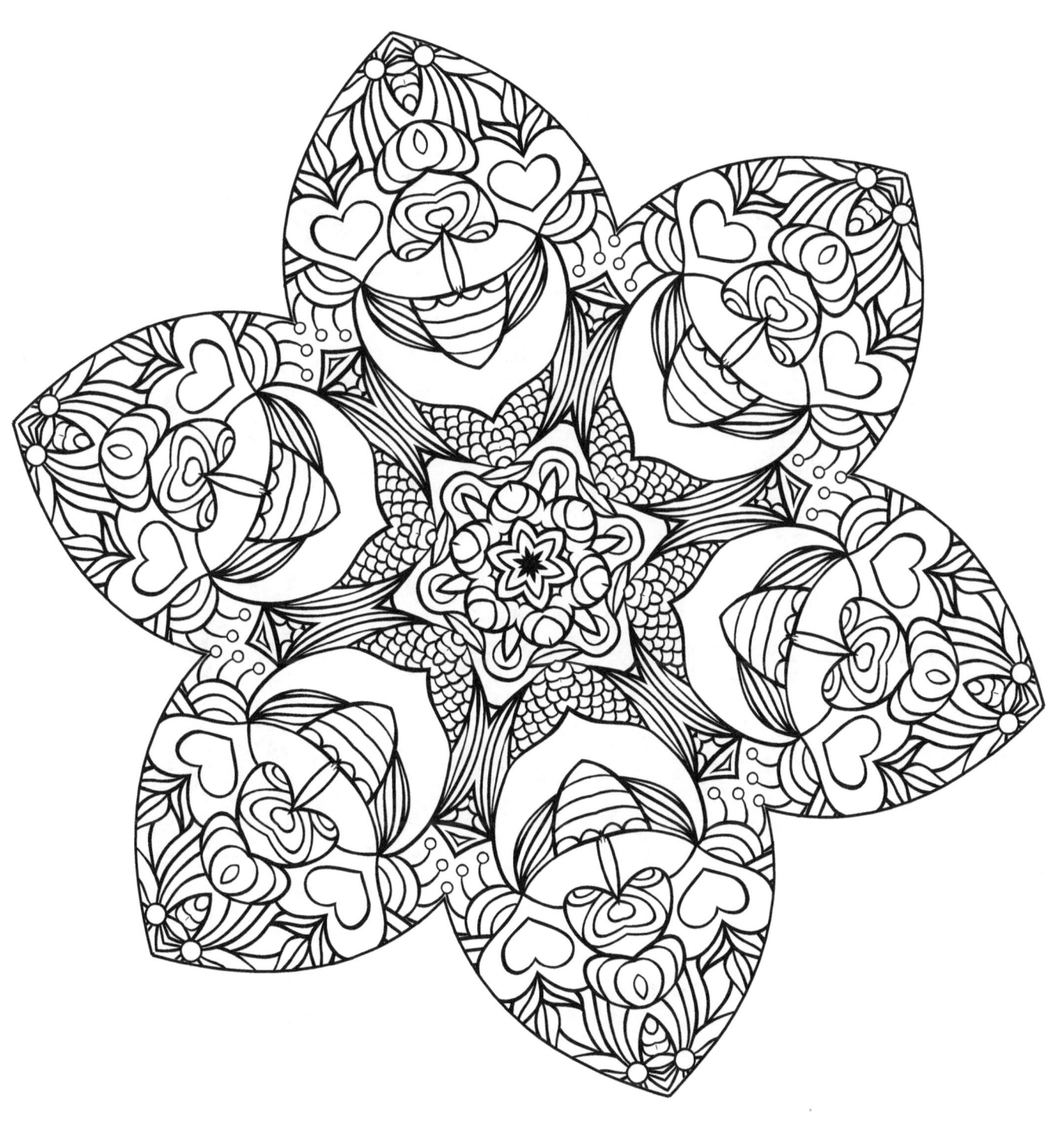

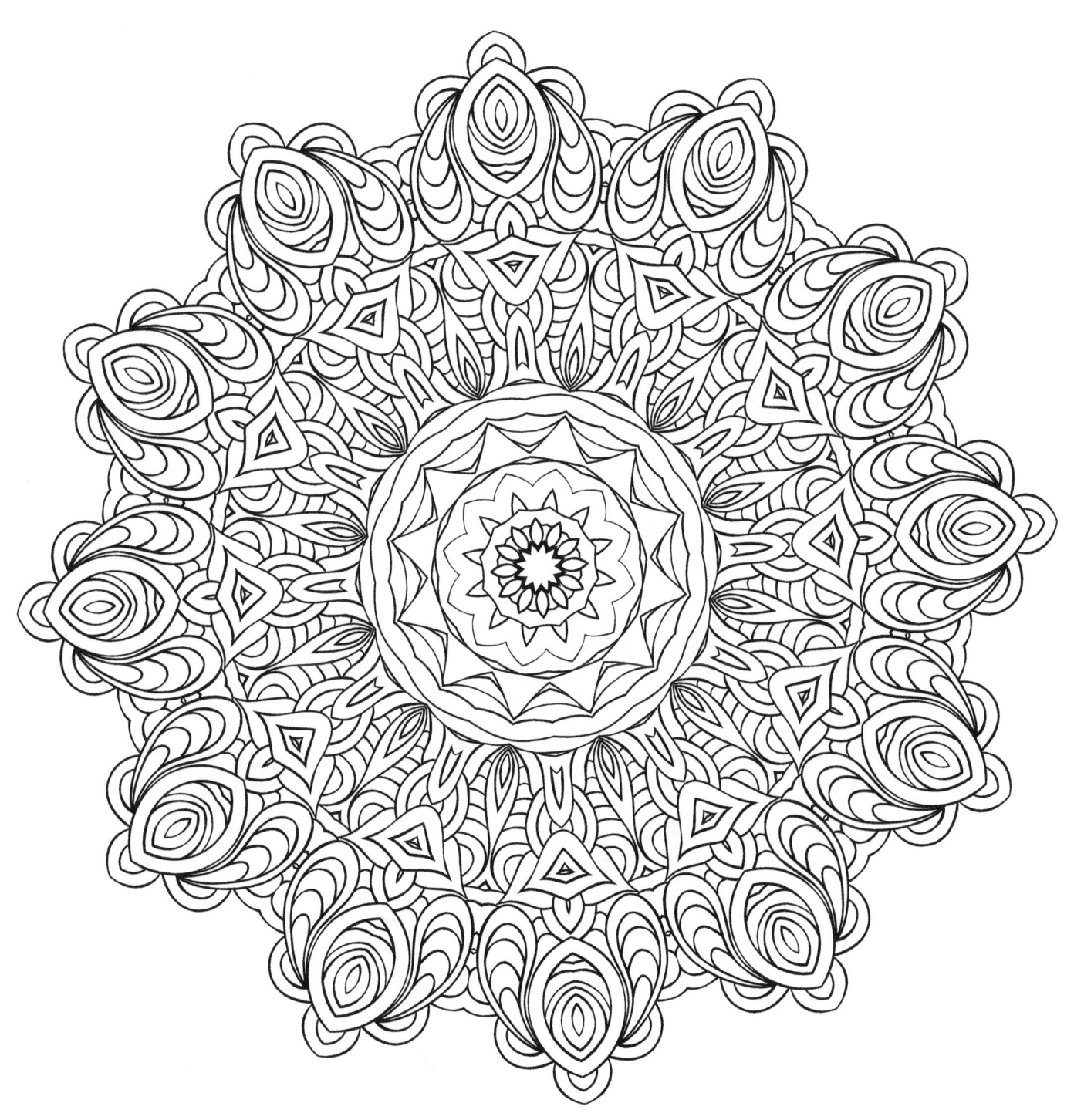

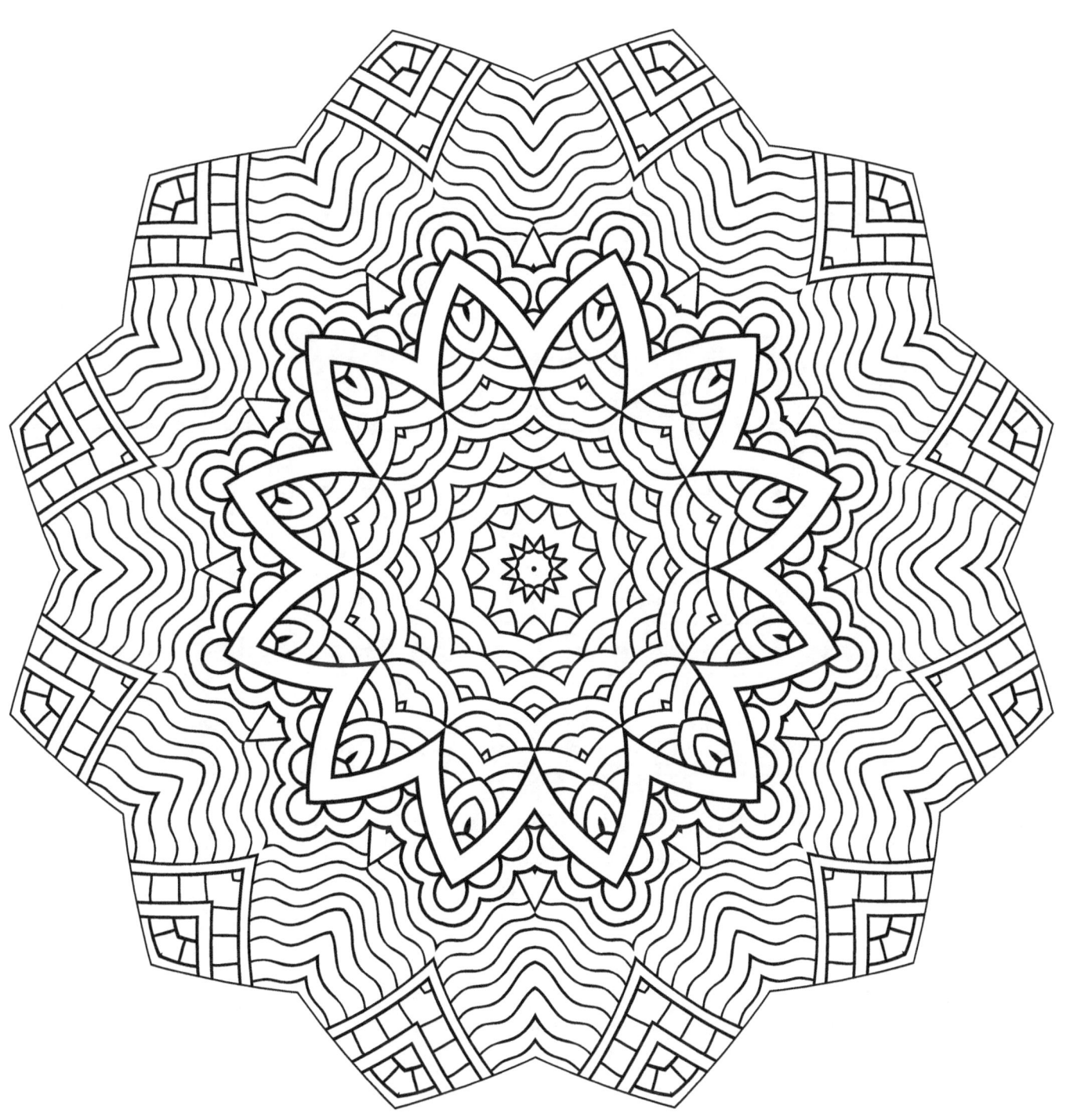

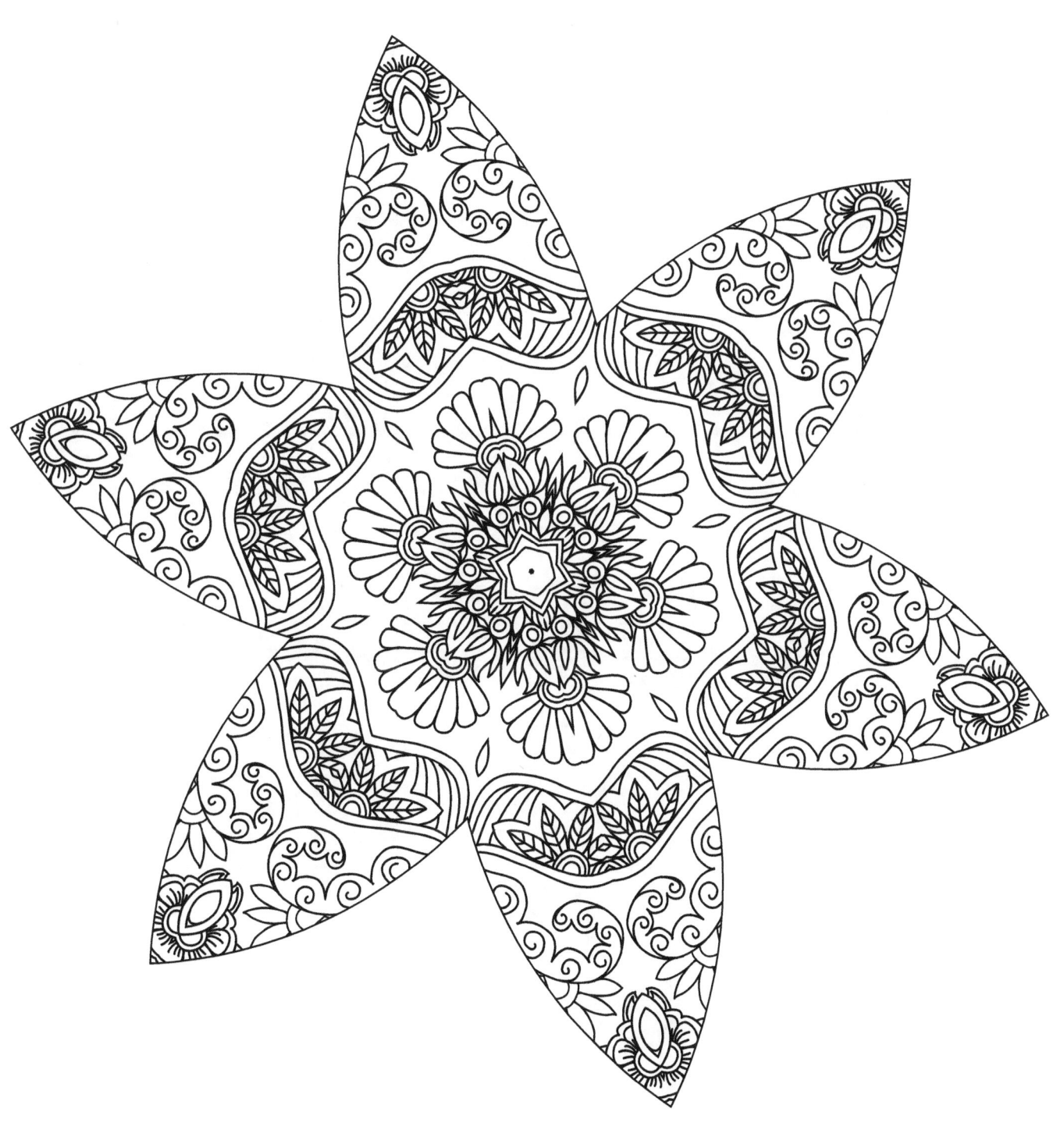

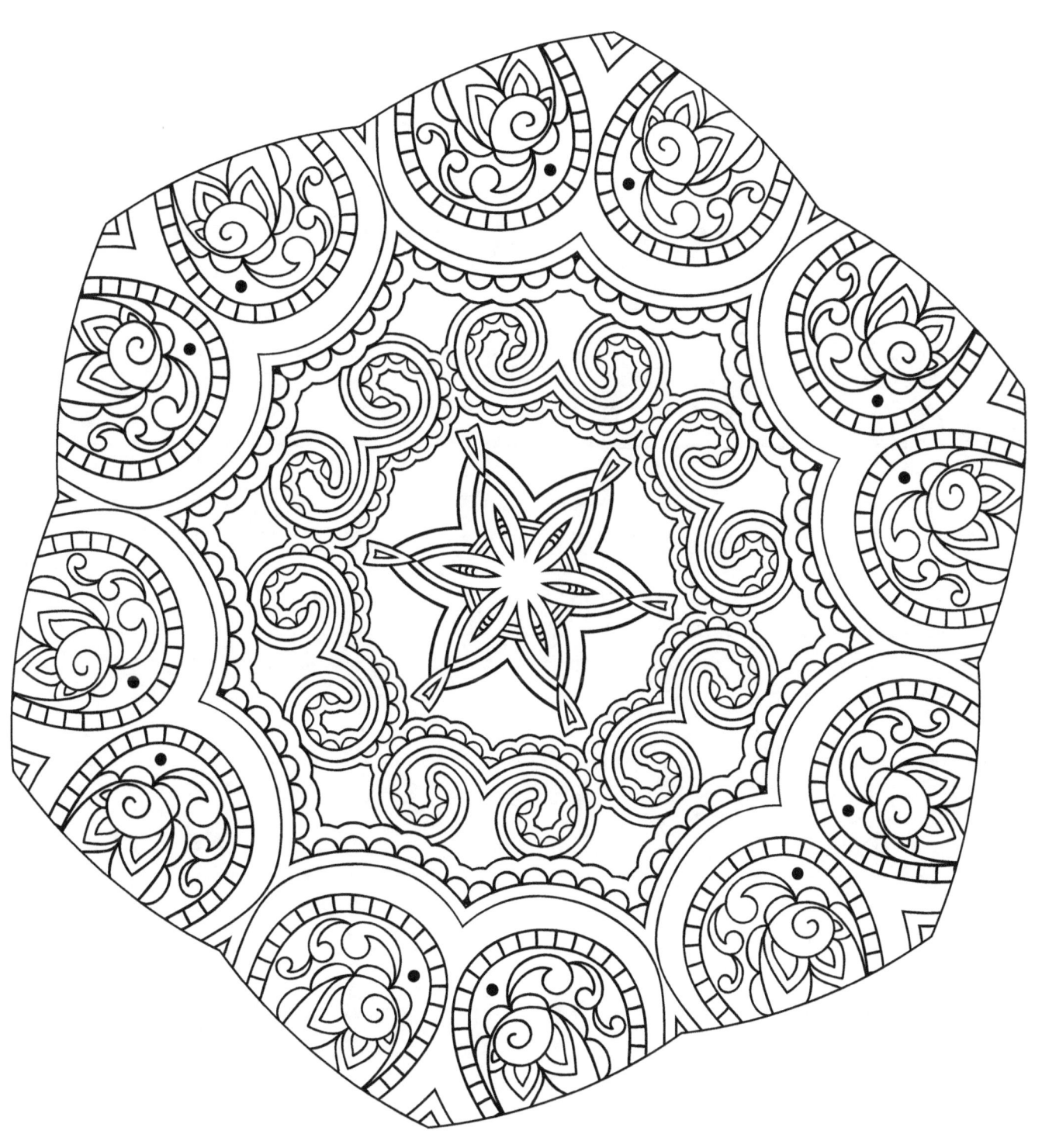

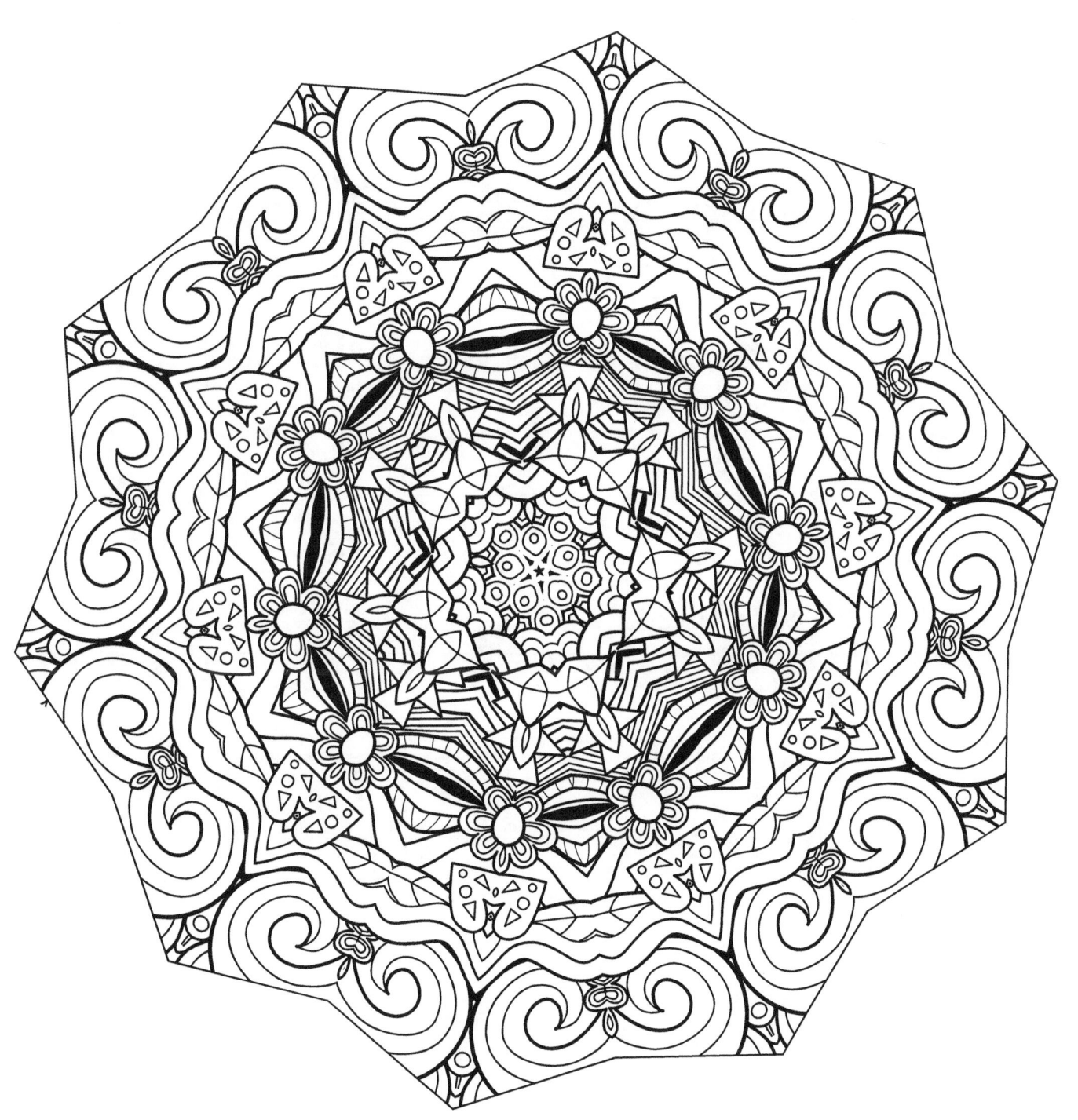

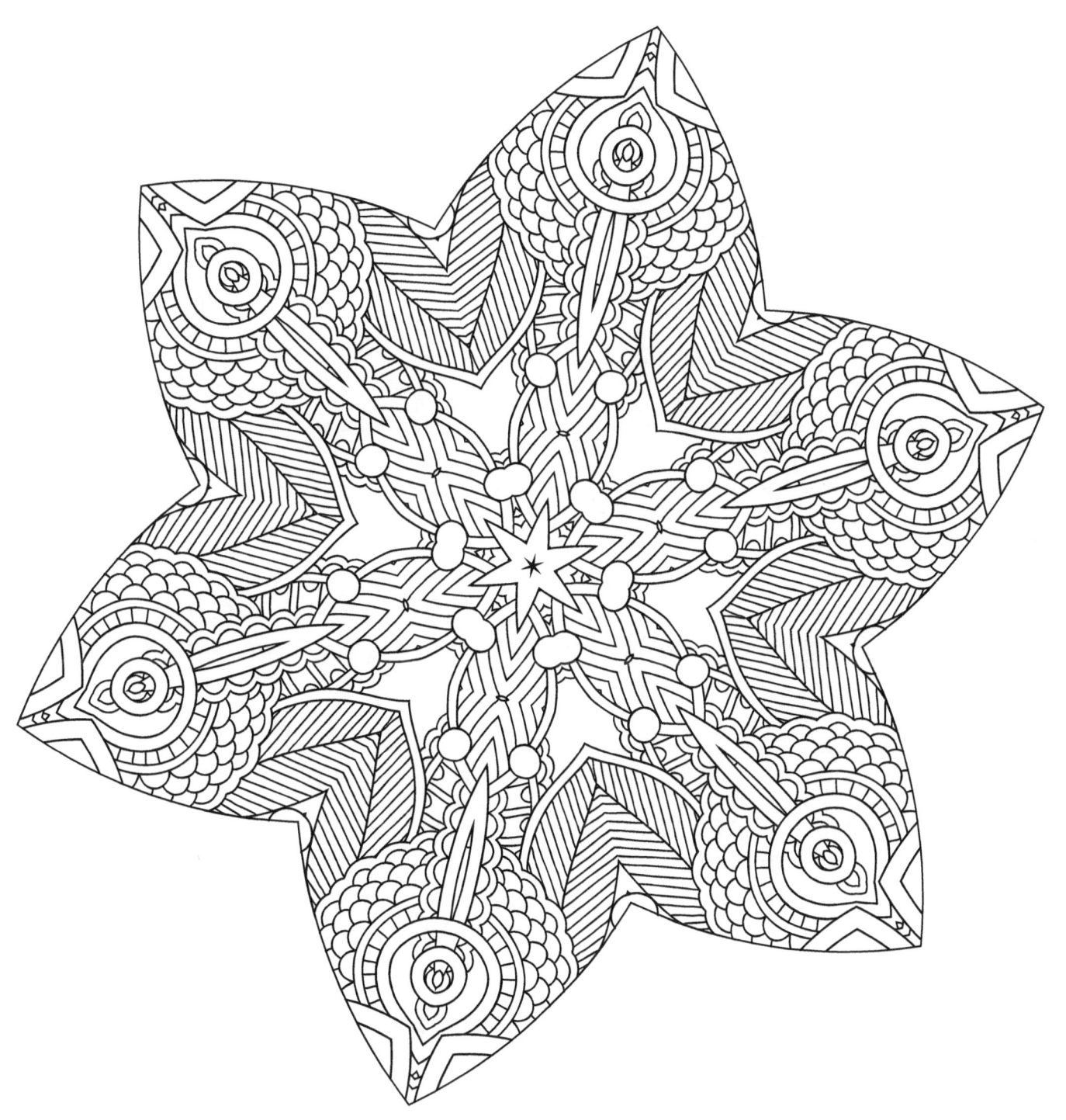

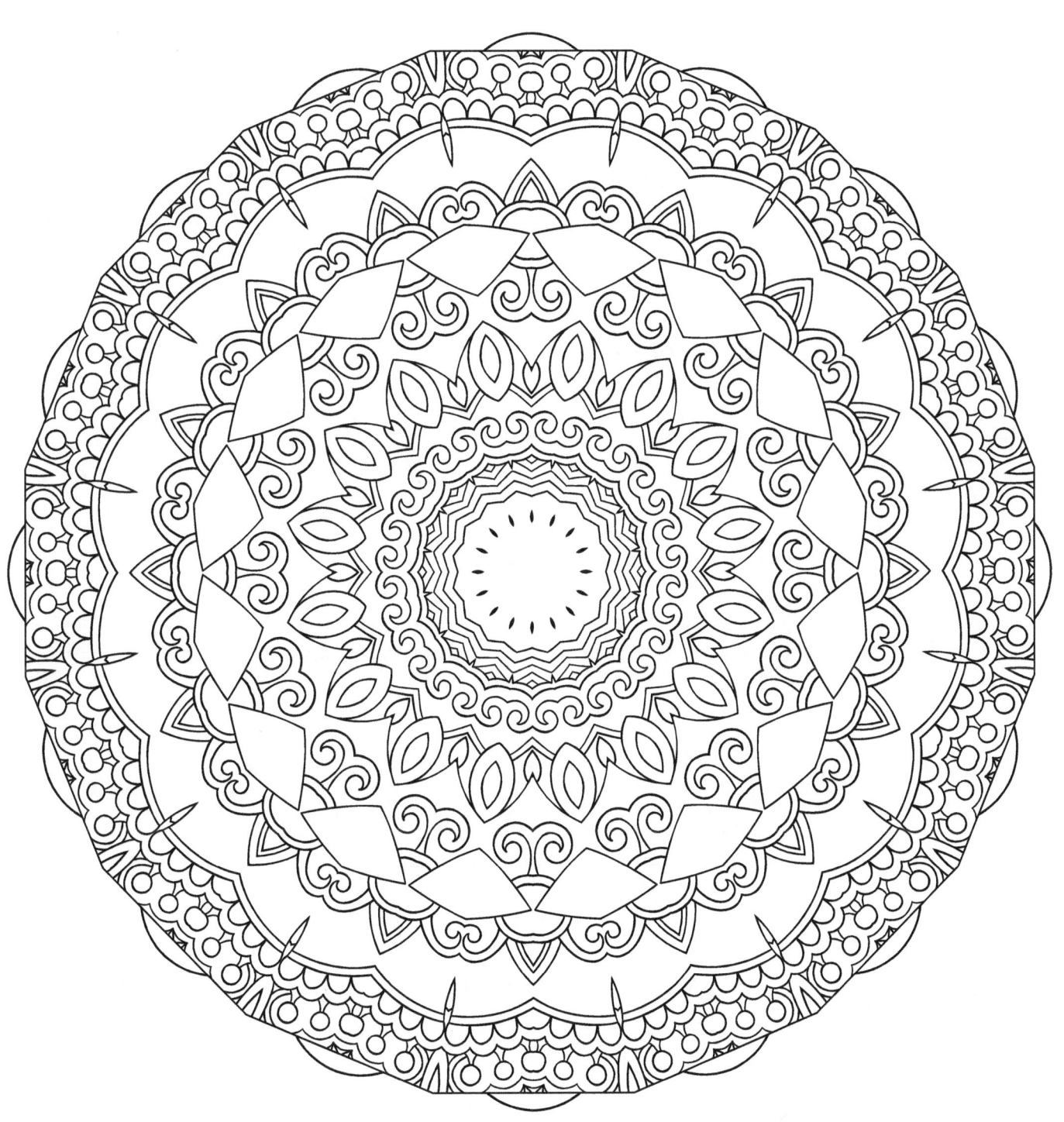

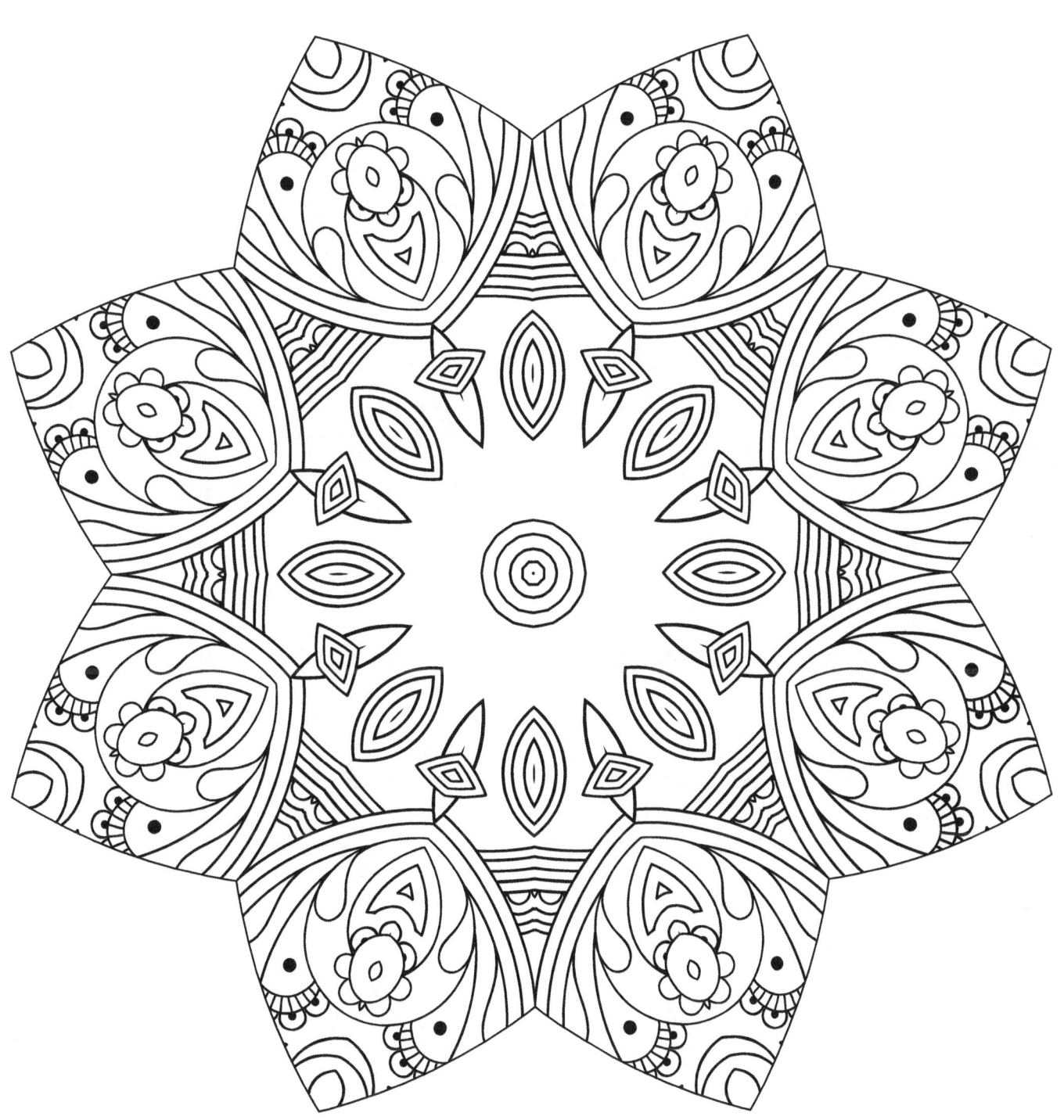

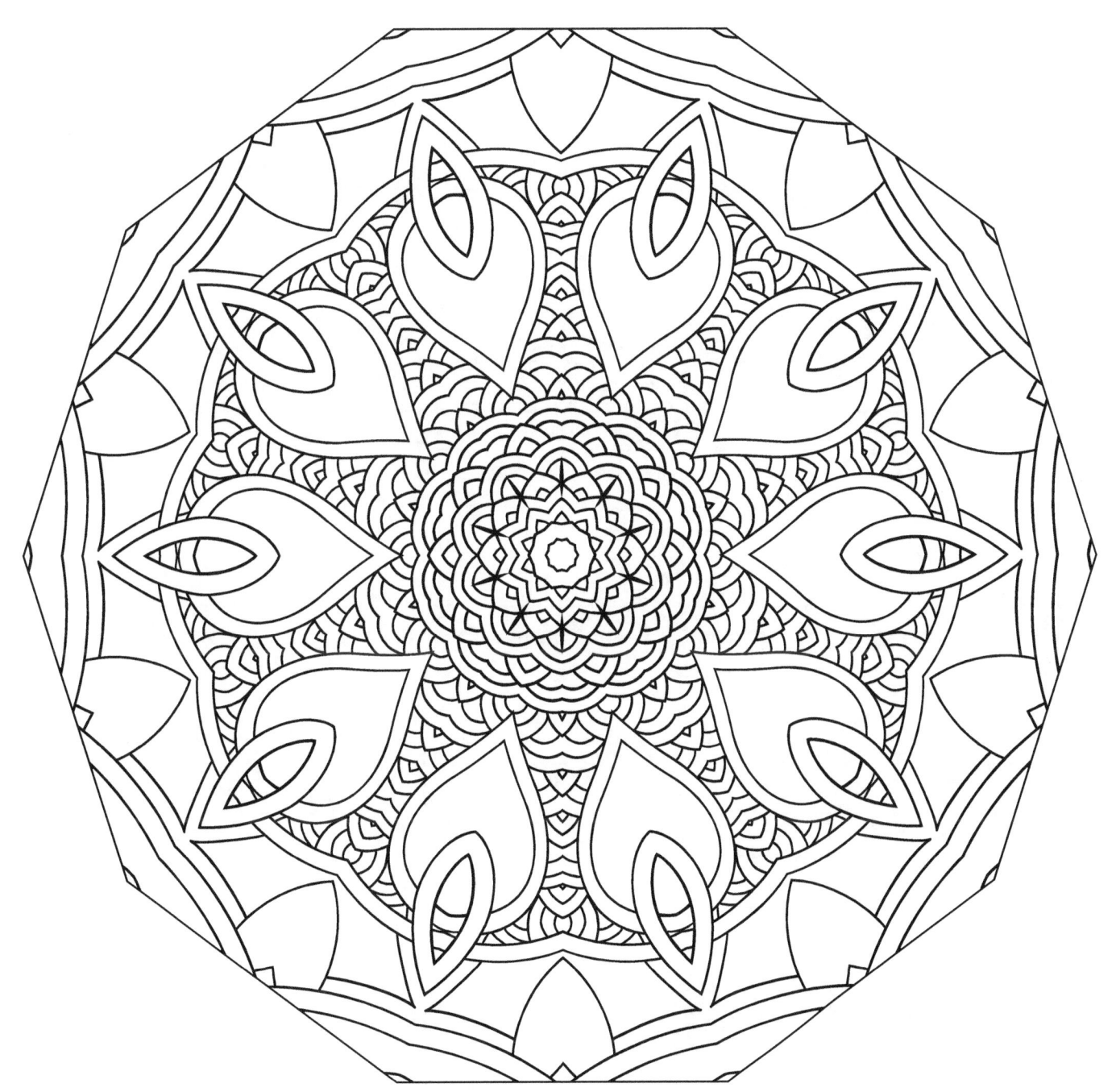

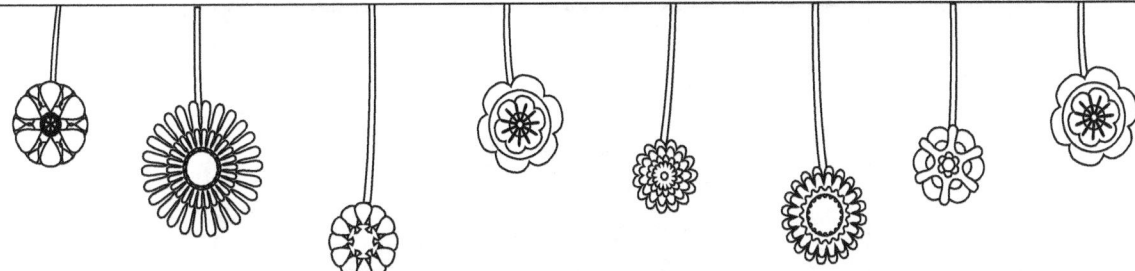
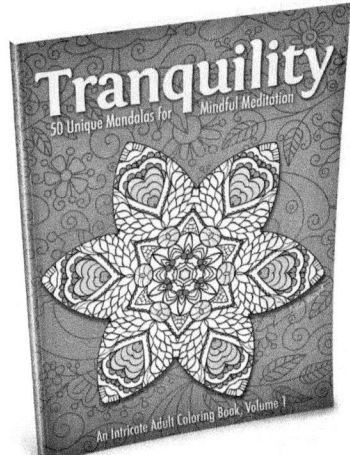
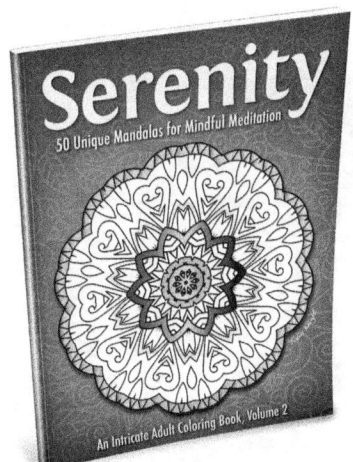
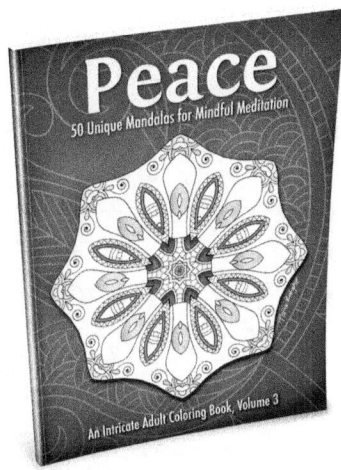
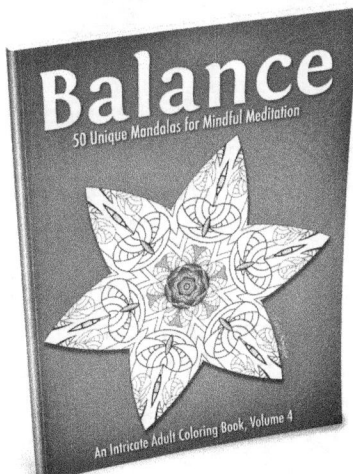
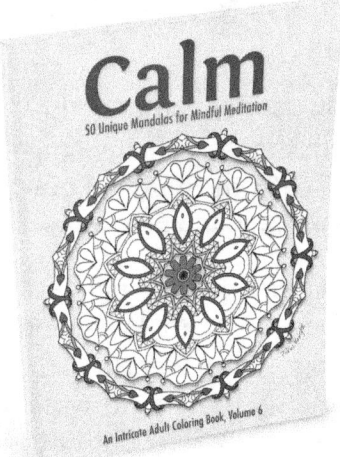

ABOUT THE AUTHOR

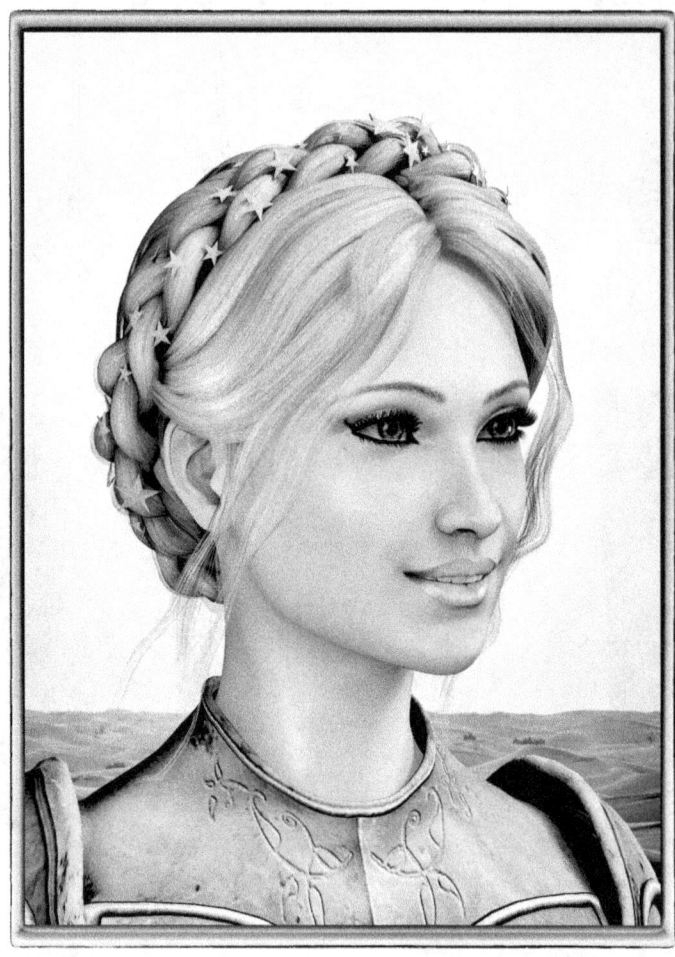

Talia Knight is the pen name of the author/artist. She is a prolific reader, and when she was faced with the task of choosing a pen name, she knew just where to turn. She chose "Talia" because it's the name of one her favorite fantasy heroines, and "Knight" because she loves sword and sorcery fantasy.

Of course, once she had the name, she had to create a picture worthy of her new fantasy-inspired alter ego. What could be more appropriate than a strong female (she has to be strong—she's wearing all that armor!) trekking through the desert with perfect hair and absolutely no sweat dripping down her face? Her makeup isn't even smudged. Realistically, she ought to be laid out flat on that sand, red as a lobster with heatstroke.

On a more serious note, Talia considers herself the luckiest person in the world because she has the privilege of helping to care for her handicapped sister while living in the great state of Texas. When she's not spending time with her sister or playing with her many nieces and nephews, she's usually doing something with books. Creating, writing, editing, selling—you name it, she's probably done it.

Get your free, print-quality PDF edition today:

Flip to the last page of this book and type in the download link into your web browser. Once you enter your email address, a link to your PDF edition of *Calm: 50 Mandalas for Mindful Meditation* will be emailed to you. That's all there is to it.

As a bonus, you will receive **an exclusive, free coloring page every week** from me that I will never share anywhere else.

Once you receive your PDF edition, you can print out as many copies as you'd like of any mandala in this book for your personal use or for your family's use.

What can I do with a PDF of this coloring book?

There are lots of different reasons you may want more than one copy of a mandala. What if you decide you don't like your color scheme and you want to start over? Or what if you want to try a bunch of different coloring techniques on the same image to see what it looks like?

Sometimes it's easier to give yourself permission to unleash your creativity when you can print off another copy if you don't like the result. But it's not practical to order a new coloring book each time you want a copy of one particular mandala. That's what the PDF edition is for.

A fun gift idea is to print one of these mandalas on specialty paper, color it, and frame it as a special present for a loved one.

There is no right or wrong way to use this book:

Color in the lines, or don't. Choose the color scheme that suits you best, using one color or dozens. Use shading if you want, or no shading at all. You are the artist here, and this is your book. Use it as you like.

When using markers or gel pens, place a piece of white printer paper underneath the mandala you are coloring. This will prevent possible bleed-through onto your next design.

A scratch page is provided at the end of the book:

The scratch page provided on the last page of this book is for testing your markers, gel pens, and color combinations. Feel free to use the download link page as a scratch page as well.

BENEFITS YOU CAN RECEIVE FROM COLORING

Achieve Mindfulness: Coloring is like yoga for the mind; it promotes centering, balance, and a focus on the present. Mindfulness can be achieved through coloring, since it also involves intentionally focusing on the present. An overall sense of well-being can be experienced as a result of mindfulness.

Experience Flow: Coloring intricate and abstract mandalas is uniquely suited to help you achieve flow, a state where you are completely immersed in the coloring experience to the point that time, space, and self are not interrupting the present moment. Experiencing flow tends to produce intense feelings of relaxation and enjoyment.

Balance: Both sides of your brain are activated when coloring: the logic side as you work within the structure of the coloring pages, and your creative side as you choose how you want to color within that structure.

Calm: The amygdala—a tiny region in your brain—plays a big role in identifying threats and producing a fight or flight response in your body. Coloring gives your amygdala a break because it helps center your brain. When your amygdala gets a break, you feel more calm and tranquility, and less anxiety. More peace and serenity, and less fear.

Meditation: Coloring is a form of active meditation. Many people have difficulty with traditional forms of meditation that require a still body and mind. The repetitive actions required in coloring abstract, geometric designs helps focus the brain on the present while blocking out intrusive thoughts.

Replace negative thoughts with positive: Since the repetitive actions of coloring help you focus on the present, negative thoughts associated with past actions or the future have a harder time intruding.

Reduce anxiety: Looking at the designs on your coloring page, identifying edges and patterns, and deciding on colors all occupy the same parts of the brain that produce anxiety-related mental imagery. By focusing on coloring, you are reducing your brain's ability to engage in thought patterns that increase anxiety.

De-stress: This is what happens when anxiety decreases, calmness increases, and positive thoughts replace negative thoughts. Coloring—particularly coloring abstract, geometric patterns such as mandalas—provides the perfect escape from the daily stresses we all encounter, helping you feel both de-stressed and rejuvenated.

DOWNLOAD LINK
GET YOUR PDF DOWNLOAD LINK HERE

TranquilityColoring.com/relax-7839

Scratch Page

Test your gel pens, markers, or other mediums here to ensure they're working properly. Or try out your color combinations. Or doodle. Whatever you want - this page is for you.